Street by Street

READING

HENLEY-ON-THAMES, WOKINGHAM

Caversham, Earley, Goring, Pangbourne, Shinfield, Sonning Common, Theale, Tilehurst, Twyford, Wargrave

1st edition May 2001

© Automobile Association Developments Limited 2001

This product includes map data licensed from Ordnance Survey® with the permission of the Controller of Her Majesty's Stationery Office. © Crown copyright 2000. All rights reserved. Licence No: 399221.

Published by AA Publishing (a trading name of Automobile Association Developments Limited, whose registered office is Norfolk House, Priestley Road, Basingstoke, Hampshire, RG24 9NY. Registered number 1878835).

Mapping produced by the Cartographic Department of The Automobile Association.

ISBN 0 7495 2617 3

A CIP Catalogue record for this book is available from the British Library.

Printed by Edicoes ASA, Oporto, Portugal

The contents of this atlas are believed to be correct at the time of the latest revision. However, the publishers cannot be held responsible for loss occasioned to any person acting or refraining from action as a result of any material in this atlas, nor for any errors, omissions or changes in such material. The publishers would welcome information to correct any errors or omissions and to keep this atlas up to date. Please write to Publishing, The Automobile Association, Fanum House, Basing View, Basingstoke, Hampshire, RG21 4EA.

Ref: ML055

Key to map pages	ii-iii
Key to map symbols	iv-1
Enlarged scale pages	2-3
Street by Street	4-71
Index – towns & villages	72
Index – streets	73-83
Index – featured places	83-84

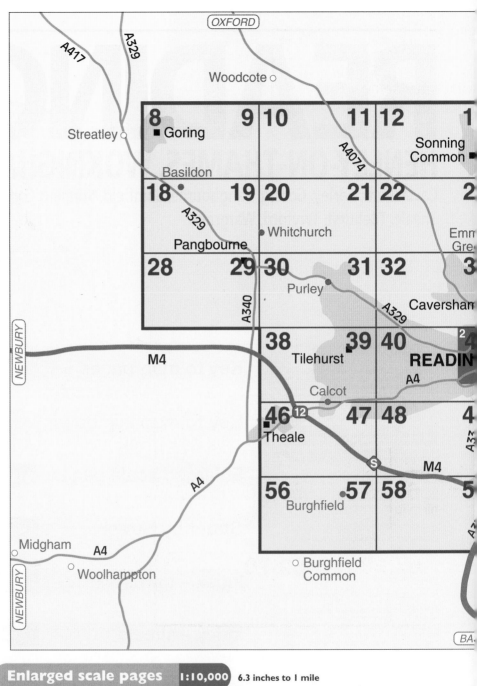

OXFORD

A417

A329

Woodcote ○

| 8 ■ Goring | 9 | 10 | 11 | 12 | 1 |

Streatley ○

A4074

Sonning Common ■

Basildon

| 18 ● | 19 | 20 | 21 | 22 | 2 |

A329

Whitchurch ●

Emm Gre

Pangbourne

| 28 | 29 30 | 31 | 32 | 3 |

A340

Purley ●

A329

Caversham

| 38 | 39 40 |

NEWBURY

M4

Tilehurst

2 4

READIN

A4

Calcot ●

| 46 12 | 47 | 48 | 4 |

Theale ■

A33

S

M4

| 56 ● 57 | 58 | 5 |

Burghfield

A4

Midgham ○

A4

Woolhampton ○

○ Burghfield Common

NEWBURY

BA

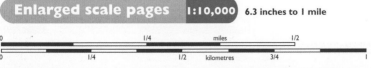

Enlarged scale pages **1:10,000** 6.3 inches to 1 mile

| 0 | 1/4 | miles | 1/2 |

| 0 | 1/4 | 1/2 | kilometres | 3/4 | 1 |

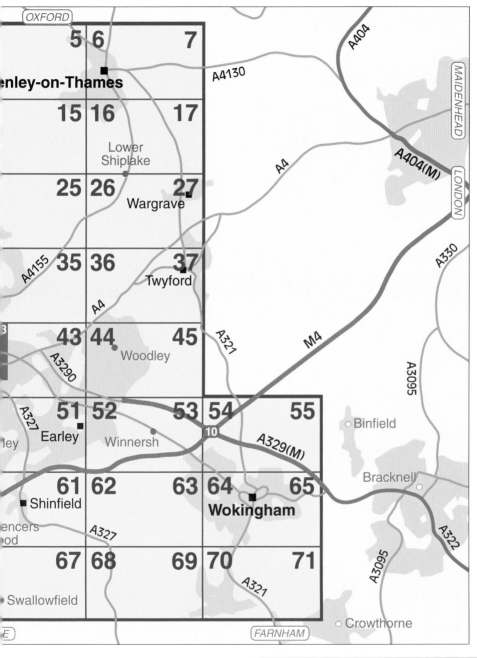

OXFORD

5 | 6 | 7

...nley-on-Thames

A4130

A404

MAIDENHEAD

15 | 16 | 17

Lower
Shiplake

A4

A404(M)

LONDON

25 | 26 | 27

Wargrave

35 | 36 | 37

A4155

Twyford

A4

A330

43 | 44 | 45

A3290

Woodley

A321

M4

A327

A3095

51 | 52 | 53 | 54 | 55

Earley

Winnersh

10

A329(M)

Binfield

Bracknell

61 | 62 | 63 | 64 | 65

Shinfield

Wokingham

...encers
...od

A327

A3095

A322

67 | 68 | 69 | 70 | 71

Swallowfield

A321

Crowthorne

...E

FARNHAM

4.2 inches to 1 mile **Scale of main map pages** 1:15,000

| 0 | 1/4 | miles | 1/2 | 3/4 | 1 |

| 0 | 1/4 | 1/2 | kilometres 3/4 | 1 | 1 1/4 | 1 1/2 |

Junction 9	Motorway & junction	**P+**🚌	Park & Ride
Services	Motorway service area	🚌	Bus/Coach station
	Primary road single/dual carriageway	⇄	Railway & main railway station
Services	Primary road service area	⇄	Railway & minor railway station
	A road single/dual carriageway	⊖	Underground station
	B road single/dual carriageway	⊖	Light Railway & station
	Other road single/dual carriageway	++++++++++	Preserved private railway
	Restricted road	LC	Level crossing
	Private road	•—•—•—•	Tramway
← ←	One way street	------------	Ferry route
	Pedestrian street	....	Airport runway
============	Track/ footpath	— · — · — · —	Boundaries- borough/ district
▮▮▮▮▮▮▮▮	Road under construction	ⱽⱽⱽⱽⱽⱽⱽⱽ	Mounds
[- - = = {	Road tunnel	**93**	Page continuation 1:15,000
P	Parking	**7**	Page continuation to enlarged scale 1:10,000

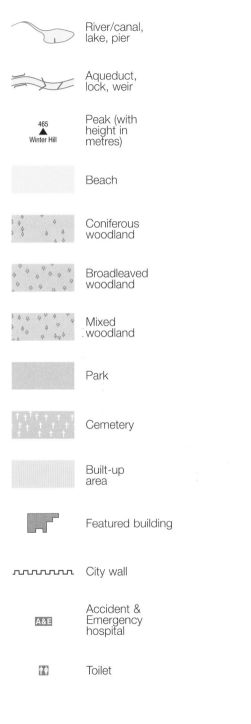

River/canal, lake, pier	Toilet with disabled facilities
Aqueduct, lock, weir	Petrol station
465 Winter Hill — Peak (with height in metres)	PH — Public house
Beach	PO — Post Office
Coniferous woodland	Public library
Broadleaved woodland	Tourist Information Centre
Mixed woodland	Castle
Park	Historic house/ building
Cemetery	Wakehurst Place NT — National Trust property
Built-up area	M — Museum/ art gallery
Featured building	Church/chapel
City wall	Country park
A&E — Accident & Emergency hospital	Theatre/ performing arts
Toilet	Cinema

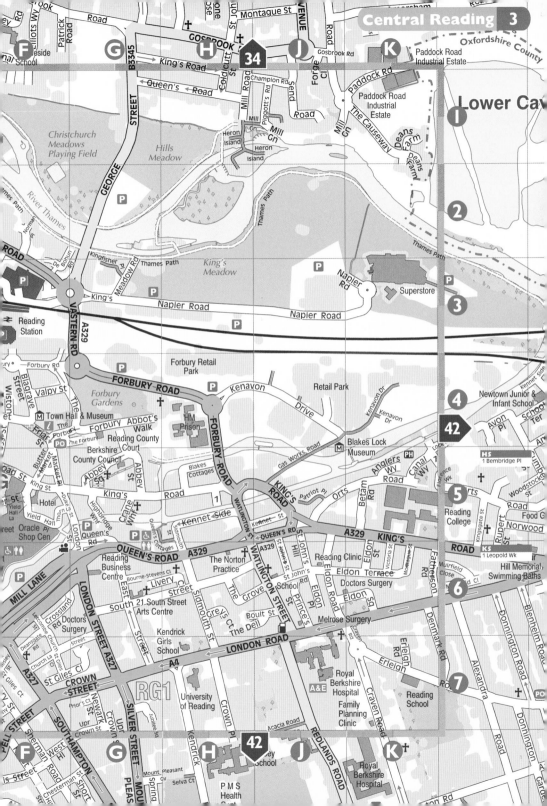

4

Ⓐ Ⓑ Ⓒ Ⓓ

Manor Farm

Brawns House

Lawrence's Farm

Bromsden Farm

Lambr
Wo

1

Rockylane Farm

2

Broadp

Green

Greys Court 🏳
(NT)

3

Rocky Lane

Greys Green

4

Bolt's Cross

5

Church Cl

✝

**Rotherfield
Greys**

Dog Lane

Ⓐ Ⓑ **14** Ⓒ Ⓓ

Crosslanes

Cowfields F

Lower Assendon

PH

E F G H

Six Hill

Hill

The Grove

FAIR

Oxfordshire Way

I

Fair Mile

Fairies Hole

The Mount

2

Lambridge Wood Road

MILE

Barn La

New Farm

Lambridge Lane

Bowling ct

Clements Rd

Luker

Pryce's orch

3

Abrahams Rd

Cooper

Crisp

6

Avenue

Lei

Badgemore House

Road

Mount

Badgemore CP School

Hop Gdns

Clar

Townlands Hospital

The Bell Surg

Lower Hernes

The Hart Surg

The West Street Practice

4

Park'side

Pack And Prime La

Ancastle Gn

Milton Cl

Deanfie

Road

The Henley College

Paradise Road

Leaver Rd

Deanfield Road

Tilebarn Cl

Laud's Cl

Anne's St.

5

Elizabeth Cl

Harcourt Cl

Sacred Heart RC School

Hernes

Haywards Cl

HE ON-

Hernes Estate

E F **15** G H

Two Tree Hl

Valley

Chiltern Cl

Gainsborough Cr's

Knappe Cl

Gainsborough Hill

The

St Mary's Cl

Elizabeth Cl

Craven Pel an

Kingwood Cres

James Way

Sherwood Gdns

Gainsborough Road

Greys Road

St.

Nichola's Road

Road

Primary School

Chalcraft Cl

Auton Creek

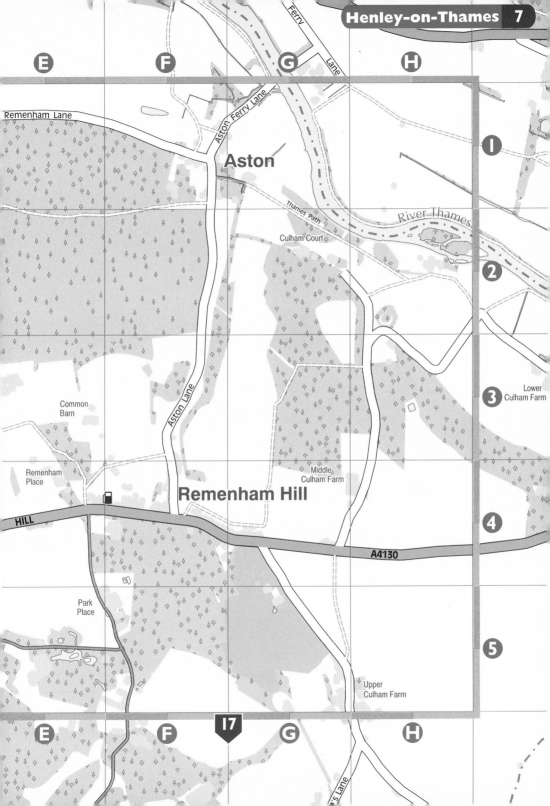

E F G H

I

Ferry Lane

Aston Ferry Lane

Remenham Lane

Aston

Thames Path

River Thames

2

Culham Court

Aston Lane

Lower
Culham Farm

3

Common
Barn

Remenham
Place

Middle
Culham Farm

Remenham Hill

HILL

4

A4130

Park
Place

5

Upper
Culham Farm

E F **17** G H

Street Farm

Beech Lane

E

F

Beech Farm **G**

H

Beech Lane

Wroxhills Wood

Elmorepark Wood

I

Beech Lan

Battle Road

Elvendon Priory

Elvendon Lan

Fox Co

2

Park Wood

B4526

3

10

C

Flint Ho

Great Chalk Wood

4

Upper Gatehampton Farm

Stapnall's Farm

Cold Harbour

Prepa

5

E

F

19

G

H

B471

Thames Path

Coombe End Farm

South Stoke Road

LANE

West Farm

Behoes Lane

Church Farm

Ashmore Lane

Health Cen.

A

B

Reading

C

Road

D

Woodcote CP School

Secondary School

Woodcote

The Oratory School

PO

Gap Way

1

Beech Lane

Wood La

Beech La

ROAD

Chiltern

Whitehouse

The Close

7

Wk

Ashlee

5

Lackmore Gdns

Greenmoor

The Oratory School

1

W. Chiltern

Bridle Path

4

11

10

Grimmer

8

3

6

9

Croft Way

I

Fox Covert

Greenmoor Hill

Elvendon Lane

Green La

2

GORING

Shirvell's Hill

Potklin Lane

Eastfield Lane

B471

3

9

Cray's Pond

1

B4526

Long Toll

4

Great Oaks

The Oratory Preparatory School

5

B471

A

B

20

Bottom

C

D

Hocketts Cl

Hill Bottom

Rivacres

Goring Heath

Corkel's Farm

Heath End

E   F   G   Beechwood Farm   H

Exlade Street

PH

Hookend

Lower Farm

Lane

Hook End

I

Rumerhedge Wood

Lackmore Wood

2

Nipper Grove

College or Abbot's Wood

Park Lane

3

12

DEADMAN'S LANE   B4526

4

A4074

Kempwood

Abbotsfield

5

Alnut's Hospital

Deadman's

Lane

E   F   21   G   N Hey Green   H   Ca

En

12

A   B   C   D

Beechwood
Farm

1

Rumerhedge
Wood

Wyfold
Grange

Wyfold Lane

2

Nippers
Grove

New
Copse

3

II

Gallowstree
Common

Withy
Copse

The Hamlet

Woodside
La

Hearns
La

4

D4
1 Orchard Fld

Kempwood

Horsepond Road

1

5

A4074

Wood Lane

Ha

READING ROAD

uney
Green

A   Cane
End

Cane
End Farm

B

22

C

D

Kidm

1 grid square represents 500 metres

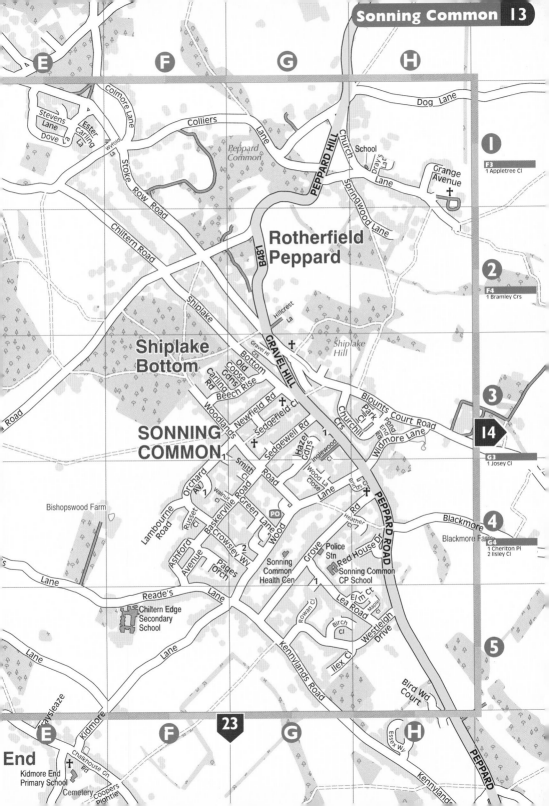

E **F** **G** **H**

Dog Lane

Stevens Lane
Ester Carling La
Dove La
Colmore Lane
Wyfold La
Colliers Lane
Peppard Common
PEPPARD HILL
Church Lane
School
Drays La
Grange Avenue

I

F3
1 Appletree Cl

Stoke Row Road
Chiltern Road
Springwood Lane

Rotherfield Peppard

B481

Shiplake

Hillcrest La

2

F4
1 Bramley Crs

Shiplake Bottom

GRAVEL HILL
Gravel Hl
Bottom
Old Copse Gdns
Carling Rd
Beech Rise
Woodlands
Newfield Rd
Sedgefield Cl
Shiplake Hill

3

SONNING COMMON

Smith Road
Sedgewell Rd
Hazel Gdns
Inglewood
Wood La
Wood Close
Churchill Crs
Park End
Blounts Court Road
Widmore Lane
Brinds

14

G3
1 Josey Cl

Bishopswood Farm

Orchard Av
Walnut Cl
Russet Cl
Green Lane
Wood
PO
Grove
Lane
Heather Cl
Red House Dr
Blackmore
Blackmore Farm

4

G4
1 Cheriton Pl
2 Ilsley Cl

Lambourne Road
Ashford Avenue
Baskerville Rd
Crowsley Wy
Pages Orch
Sonning Common Health Cen
Reade's Lane
Police Stn
Sonning Common CP School
PEPPARD ROAD

Chiltern Edge Secondary School
Rowan Cl
Birch Cl
Lea Road
Elm Ct
Maple Cl
Westleigh Drive
Ilex Cl
Kennylands Road
Bird Wd Court

5

End

E **F** **23** **G** **H**

Graysleaze
Kidmore
Chalkhouse Gn Rd
Kidmore End Primary School
Cemetery
Coopers Pightle
Essex Wy
PEPPARD
Kennylands

14

A   B   **Rotherfield**
Grovs
4   C   D

Dog Lane

Crosslanes   Cowfields Fa

1

Grange
Avenue

2   Upper
House Farm

Kings Farm Lane

3
urt Road
e Lane   **13**   Devil's Hill   Old Place

4   more   Crowsley
Park
Blackmore Farm   Lane

5   Frieze Farm   **Crowsley**

Bird Wd
ourt

A   B   **24**   C   D

PEPPA

1 grid square represents 500 metres

E   F   **5**   G   H

Hernes

Hernes Estate

Elizabeth Close

Two Tree Hl

St Mary's Cl

Elizabeth Road

Nicholas Road

Chiltern Cl

Valley Road

Greys Road

Highlands Lane

Greys Road

Highlands Farm

Deanfield
Harcourt Cl
Haywards Cl
Sacred Heart RC School

HE
ON-

Laud's
Barn

Gravett Cr
Le Penjally
Knappe Cl
Gainsborough Crs
Gainsborough Rd
Gainsborough Hl

The Er

Greys Road

St

And

St

Green St

Manor Rd

Auton Pl

I

Primary School

Chalcraft Cl

Makins Road

Gillotts Cl

Lovell Cl

Wootton Rd

MW Cotts

Sherwood Gdns

Coldharbour Cl

St Katherine's Rd

Blandy Rd

2

Henley District Indoor Sports Centre

Gillotts School

Gillott's Lane

Harpsden Bottom

Chalk Hill

3

16

Hunt's Farm

Perseverance Hill

White Hill

Mays Green

4

Red Hill

Bellehatch Park

High Wood

5

Upp Bolr

E   F   **25**   G   H

Bones Lane

PH

E F **7** G Upper Culham Farm H

I

Coc Gree

Kenton's Lane

Hatchgate House

ROAD

Temple Combe

Wokingham

Oxfordshire County

River Thames

A321

Worley's Farm

2

C **3** zies Hill

Path

Bolney Road

Hennerton House

Mapl Croft

4

Highfield Farm

Basmore Lane

LC

Shiplake Station

Lashbrook Road

Willow

Lowes Close

Lashbrook Rd

Road

E F **27** A321 G H

5

Wargrave Manor

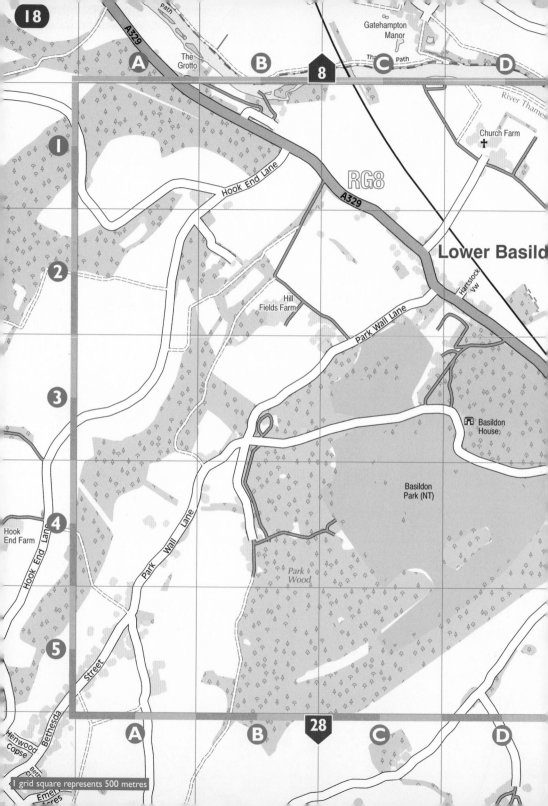

18

A329

The Grotto

A

B

8

C

Path

D

Gatehampton
Manor

River Thames

1

Church Farm

Hook End Lane

RG8

A329

Lower Basild

2

Hill
Fields Farm

Park Wall Lane

Hartslock
Vw

3

Basildon
House

4

Hook
End Farm

Park Wall Lane

Basildon
Park (NT)

Hook End Lane

5

Street

Park
Wood

Henwood
Copse

Bethesda

Emer

A

B

28

C

D

1 grid square represents 500 metres

Coombe End Farm

Beech Farm

Thames Path

Thames Path

Beale Park

The Ridge

k Farm

SHOOTER'S

HILL

Oxfordshire County

West Berkshire

Coombe Park

B471

Hardwick

Manor Road

Swanston Field

HIGH STREET

Eastfie

Whitchurch-on-Thames

Hillside

Toll

TCHURCH ROAD

Thames

Pangbourne Medical Centre

A329

Hartslock Court

Pangbourne

20

A　　　B　　　**10**　　　C　　　D

Hill Bottom

1

Hocketts Cl

Hill Bottom Cl

Rivacres

Oakdown Cl

Beech Tithe

Goring Heath

1

B1
1 Bridle Rd

B471

Orchard Coombe

Bridle Road

Whitchurch Hill

✝

2

Beech Farm

Butler's Pond

3

B471

Bozedown House

19

The Baul

4

Hillside Road

Bozedown Farm

✝ B471

Hardwick

Manor Road

Swanston Field

Whitchurch Primary School

5

Eastfield Lane

Eastfield Lane

HIGH STREET

✝

Toll

A　　　B　　　**30**　　　C　　　D

Thames Path

Wi...bury Farm

Pangbourne Medical

✝ Thames

1 grid square represents 500 metres

Abbotsfield

E

F

11

G

H

Alnut's Hospital

Nuney
Green

Ca
E

1

Deadman's

Lane

Collins
End

2

Lane

Holly
Copse

Whittles Farm

Cross Lan

3

22

Bottom
Wood

4

Bottom Farm

r Thames

5

Thames Path

E

F

31

G

Ma**H**edurham

Watermill

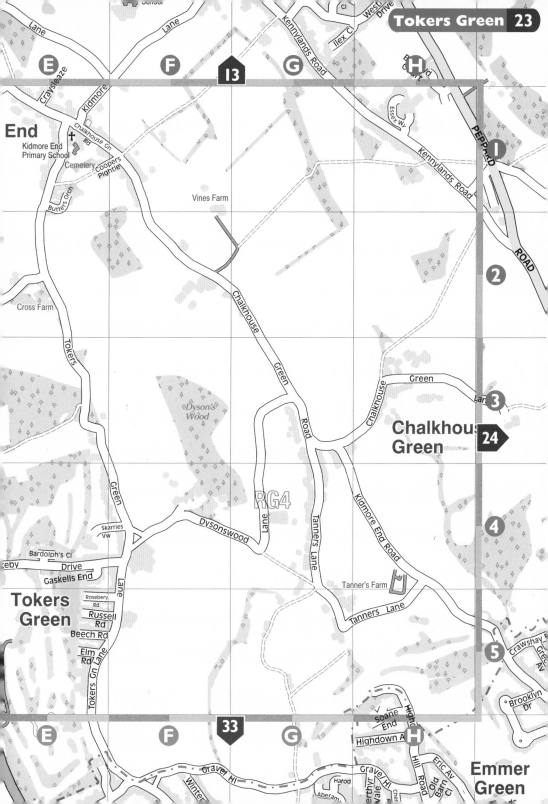

E F 13 G H

End

Crayslieze
Kidmore
Chalkhouse Cn Rd
Kidmore End
Primary School
Cemetery
Coopers Pightle
Butler's Orch
Cross Farm

Vines Farm

Tokers

Dyson's Wood

Green

Chalkhouse Green

RG4

Skarries Vw

Bardolph's Cl
...eby Drive
Gaskells End

Tokers Green

Rosebery Rd
Russell Rd
Beech Rd
Elm Rd
Tokers Gn Lane

Dysonswood

Lane

Chalkhouse Green Road

Kidmore End Road

Tanners Lane

Tanner's Farm

Tanners Lane

School
Cl
West... Drive
Ilex Cl
Kennylands Road

Essex W.
Kennylands Road

I
PEPP...D
ROAD
2

Chalkhouse Green
Lane
3

Chalkhous Green
24

4

5
Crawshay Gn
Av
Brooklyn Dr

Soane End
Highdown A
Highdown A
Hill Road
Crawshay
Eric Av
Old Barn Cl

Emmer Green

E F 33 G H

Gravel Hi
Winter...
Gravel Hi
Hafod
Aberam
Merthyr Vale
Cher

24

A **B** **14** **C** **D**

Crowsley

Frieze Farm

Bird Wd Court

1

PEPPARD

Kennylands Road

ROAD

2

B481

Green

Lane

3

Chalkhouse Green

23

A5
1 Spinney Cl

Bishopsland Farm

Comp Farm

Sandpit

Cork's Farm

4

B4
1 Aldeburgh Cl

Chalkhousegreen
Lane

Phillimore
1 Rd

Tower Cl

The Ridings

Bryant's Farm

Kiln Road

Row

Lane

5

Crawshay Dr

Greenleas
Av

Crawshay Dr

Rosehill
Park

PEPPARD

Peppard Rd

Russet Gld

Marchwood

Cherry
Cl

Autumn
Cl

Venetia
Close

Jefferson
Cl

Kiln Road

Foxhill Lane

Brooklyn
Dr

Courtenay
Dr

Burnham
Rise

ROAD

Yarnton
Cl

Wetherby
Cl

B481

A **B** **34** **C** **D**

Emmer

Highdown Hill Road

Eric Av

Twin
Oaks

Kidmore End Road

Chalgrove
Wy

Lyefield Ct

Fishers
Court

Dunster

Abingdon Drive

Fraser
Av

Elstow
Cl

Mallory
Hil

Gawl

Rowallan

Queensway

Caversham
Park

Caversham Park Road

Primary
Sch

St Martins
RC Primary School

Pendennis Av

1 grid square represents 500 metres

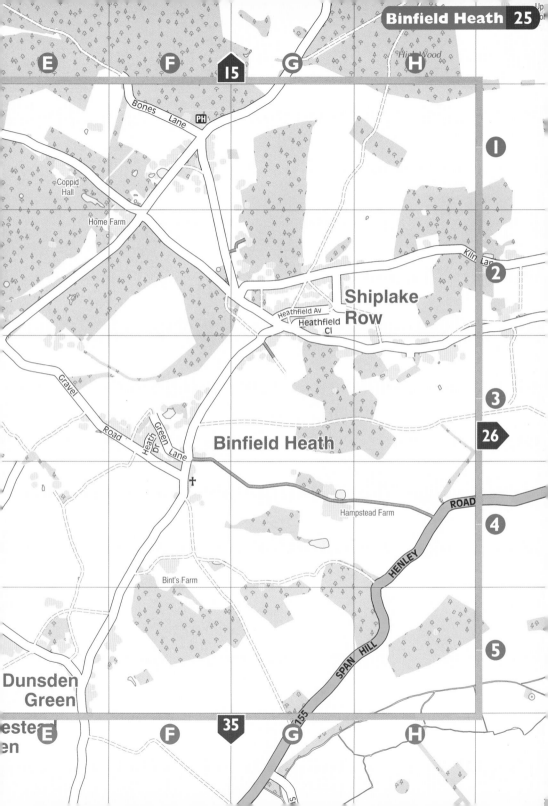

E F 15 G H

Up

I

Bones Lane

PH

Coppid Hall

Home Farm

Kiln Lane

2

Shiplake Row

Heathfield Av
Heathfield Cl

3

26

Gravel

Road

Heath Dr

Green Lane

Binfield Heath

†

Hampstead Farm

ROAD

4

HENLEY

Bint's Farm

SPAN HILL

5

Dunsden Green

esteaon

E F 35 G 155 H

S

26

A **B** **16** **C** **D**

Upper
Bolney House

Woodlands

Road

gh Wood

Bolney Trevor
Drive

Quarry
Lane

Station

Oaks

Crowsley

Blocks

Ave

Badgers

The
Chestnuts

Baskerville La

A4155

**Lower
Shiplake**

New

Road

Road

I

Kiln Lane

New Cross

Mill Lane

Avenue

2

Memorial

Orchard Cr

Shiplake

Shiplake C of E
Primary School

Plough

Plowden Wy

Lane

Church Lane

† Shiplake House

Shiplake
College

Thames Path

3

25

ROAD

4

River Thames

**Borough
Marsh**

The
Lynch

LEY

Hallsmead
Ait

5

Thames Drive

Thames Path

St Pa Bridge

A **B** **36** **C** **D**

Thames

dshire County

ng

I grid square represents 500 metres

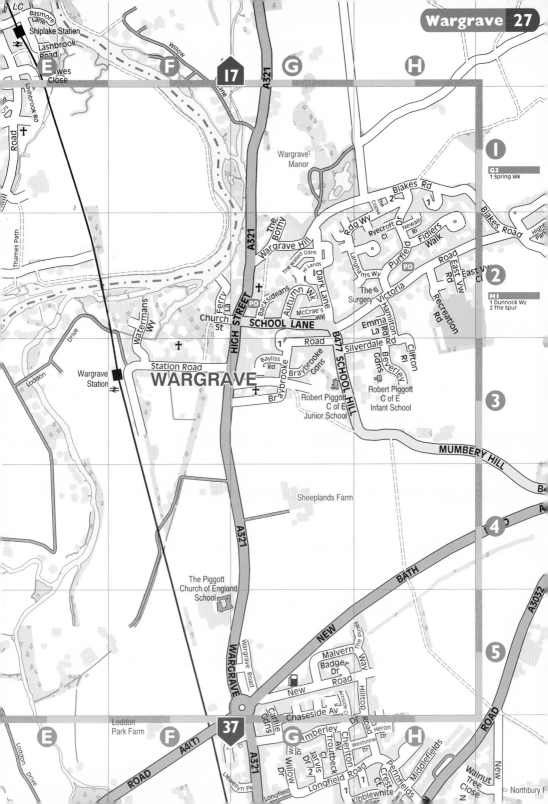

28

A B 18 C D

Bethesda Street

Henwood Copse

Bethesda Cl

1

Emery Acres

Basildon School

Woodgreen Farm   Mead Lane

Home Farm

Beckfords

Aldworth

2

Maple La

Blandy's Lane

Road

Darby La

PH

PO

✝

Pangbourne Road

New Town

Wakemans

Spring Cl

Picketts La

3

Coleridge Lane

Gardeners Lane

Upper Bowden Farm

4

5

Herons Farm

A B C Great Bear D

St Andrews School

1 grid square represents 500 metres

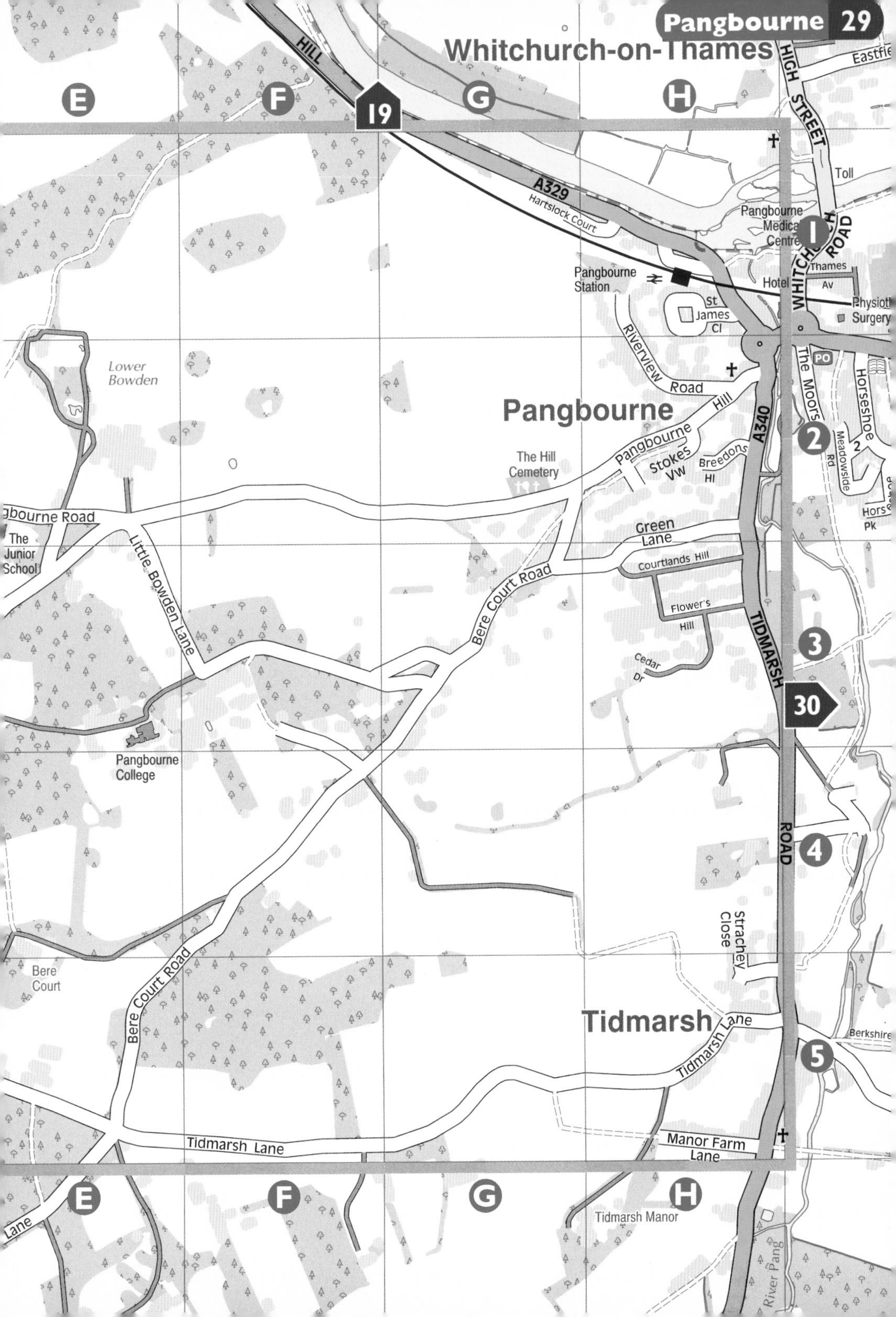

Whitchurch-on-Thames

E F 19 G H

HILL

A329

Hartslock Court

Pangbourne Station

St James Cl

Pangbourne Medical Centre

HIGH STREET

Eastfie

Toll

Thames Av

Physioth Surgery

WHITCHURCH ROAD

I

Hotel

Riverview Road

Pangbourne Hill

Pangbourne

The Hill Cemetery

Stokes VW

Breedons Hl

PO

2

The Moors

Meadowside Rd

Horseshoe

Hors Pk

A340

Green Lane

Courtlands Hill

Flower's Hill

Cedar Dr

...bourne Road

The Junior School

Little Bowden Lane

Bere Court Road

TIDMARSH

3

30

4

Strachey Close

Pangbourne College

Lower Bowden

Bere Court Road

Bere Court

Tidmarsh Lane

Tidmarsh

Tidmarsh Lane

Manor Farm Lane

Berkshire

5

ROAD

E F G H

Lane

Tidmarsh Manor

River Pang

Thames Path

E · F · **21** · G · H

Mapledurha

E4
1 Addiscombe Cha
2 Longleat Dr
3 Lucey Cl
4 Lytham End
5 Rosemead Av

I

Watermill

Mapledurham
House

Park Far

E5
1 Hawthornes
2 Kernham Dr
3 The Knoll
4 Ridgemount Cl
5 Willow Gdns

Home Farm

School

Purley Village

Lister Cl

Glebe Road

PO

Nursery Gdns

Purley Lane

Allison Gdns

New Hill

Westridge Av

Colyton Way

Wintringham Way

Brading Way

The Short

Oak Tree

WK

Chestnut Gv

River Gdns

Waterside Dr

2

St Mary's Avenue

Chiltern Vw

Thames Reach

F2
1 Hornbeam Cl
2 Primrose Cl
3 Westridge Av

Road

Sherwood Rise

Bowling Gn La

n Thames

Cecil Aldin Dr

Highfield Road

Long Lane Primary School

Long Lane

Orchard Close

Apple Close

Hazel Road

Old Farm Road

Thames Path

Skerritt Way

Marshall

F3
1 Brierley Pl
2 Duncan Gdns
3 Goodliffe Gdns
4 Huckleberry Cl
5 Huscarle Wy
6 The Hydes
7 Simons Cl

3

OXFORD ROAD

Menpes Rd

Kernham Road

A329

OXFORD

Theobald Dr

32

White Ldg Cl

Devonshire Gdns

Warley Rise

Condor Cl

Wyre Cl

Brookfields School

Westwood Farm County Junior School

Oregon Avenue

Redwood Wy

Redbuck Copse

Gwynne Close

Durant Wy

Roebuck Cl

ROAD

Tilehurst Station

F4
1 Myrtle Cl
2 Sage Rd
3 Talbot Wy

4

Knowsley

Marten

Warbreck Dr

Laytom Rise

School

Fullbrook Crs

Skilton Road

Bradwell Rd

Swinbrook Cl

Ulswater Dr

Eisley Road

Edenhall Cl

Rissington Road

Clevedon Road

Carlisle Rd

Carlisle Road

F5
1 Bowfell Cl
2 Marling Cl
3 Old Farm Crs
4 Pikeshaw Wy
5 Staddlestone Cl

Long Lane

Cranmer Cl

Downs Way

Barbara's Meadow

Conifer Cl

Conifer Dr

Clanfield Crs

Fairford Rd

Cotswold Rd

Overdown Road

Tring Rd

PO

The Surgery

Juniper Wy

Brooksby Road

Overdown Road

Road

Oak Tree Road

Western Oaks

Kentwood Hill

Rodway

Road

Grasmere

PO

5

Rydal Av

G2
1 Church Ms
2 Lilac Cl
3 Park Wk

eham Farm

Hillview Cl

Tilling Cl

Scafell Cl

Wandhope Wy

Kirkfell Cl

Dell Rd

Westwood Rd

Shipton Rd

Chepstow Rd

Elstree Rd

The Cedars

Dark Highworth Wy

Barefoot Clay

Lamorna Crs

Elder

Hartslock

Causmans Wy

Arn

Hill

Dudley Cl

Wheeler

Gipsy Lane

Vale Crescent

Rodway Road

Pottery Rd

G4
1 Barbrook Cl
2 The Beeches
3 Larkswood Cl
4 Nevis Rd

E · **H4** · **F** · **39** · G · **G5** · H

H4
1 Ferndale Cl
2 Oak Tree Copse
3 Overlanders End

Pr William Dr

Fircroft Close

Pierce's Hill

Wardle Avenue

Westwood Road Health

Armour Road

G5
1 Mapledurham Vw
2 Oakham Cl
3 Parkhill Dr
4 Southerndene Cl

Elmsto

Trelawney Dr

Five

Ivybank

Polsted Rd

Tilehurst

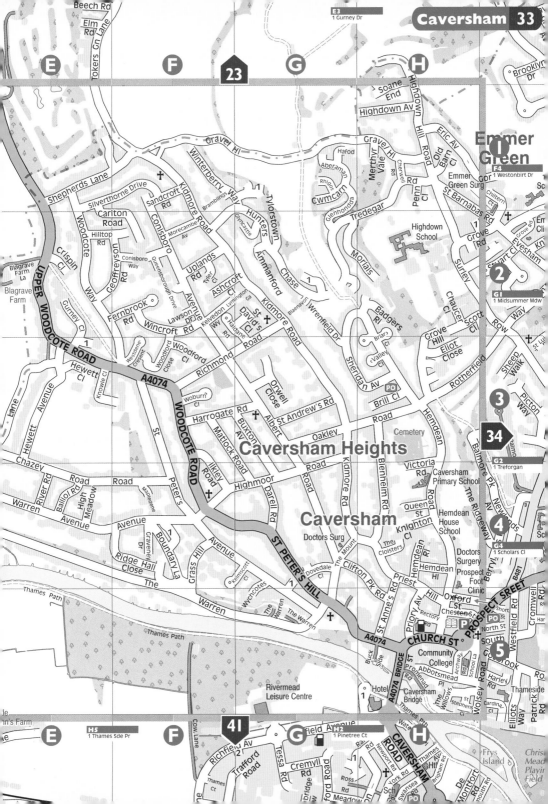

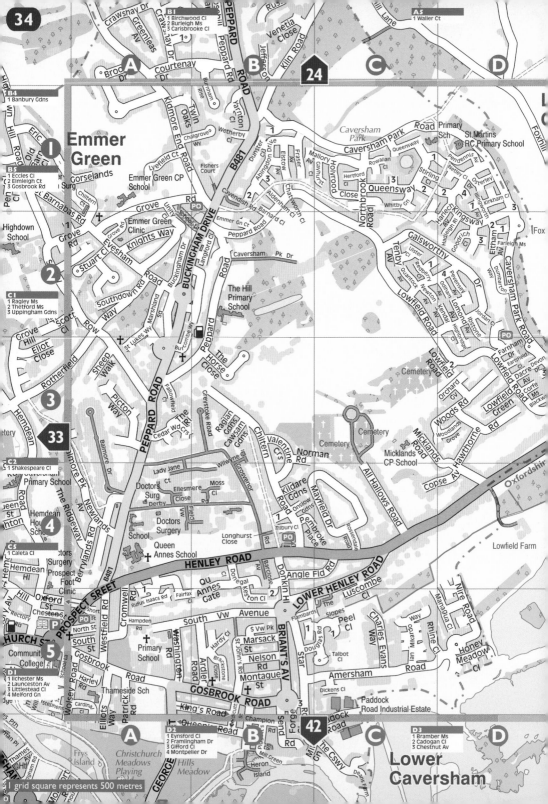

Dunsden Green

E

estead
en

F

25

G

SPAN HILL

H

A4155

I

HENLEY ROAD

Spring
Lane

A4155

**Play
Hatch**

Foxhill
Cl

B478 **PLAYHATCH ROAD**

The
Gallery M

B478

**Sonning
Eye**

2

Hotel

Thames Path

The Mill at
Sonning

3

HENLEY ROAD A4155

THAME

36

PH

High St

**PEAR
ROA**

146

4

Thames Path

Reading
Blue Coat
School

River Thames

SONNING LANE

5

Thames Path

Pkt
Holme
Farm La

E

Mari

F

43

Thames Valley
Bio s Park

G

David Lloyd
Sports
Centre

Thames Path

H

Sonning Meadows

South Dr

A4(T)

BATH ROAD

Bath

Old

BATH
ROAD

W

38

Berkshire Circular Routes

A

Sulham Lane

B

30

C

D

Manor Farm Lane

✝

1

River Pang

Sulham

✝ Sulham House

Berkshire Circular Routes

Nunhide Lane

Littl

2

D3
1 Jenner Wk

3

D4
1 The Fells
2 Mendip Dr
3 Snowden Dr

Beal's Lane

4

Malpas

Nunhide Farm

Berkshire Circular Routes

North Street

5

A

B

46

C

Nunhide Lane

M4

Pincents Lane

D

Reading Superbowl

Pincents Lane

Wickcroft

1 grid square represents 500 metres

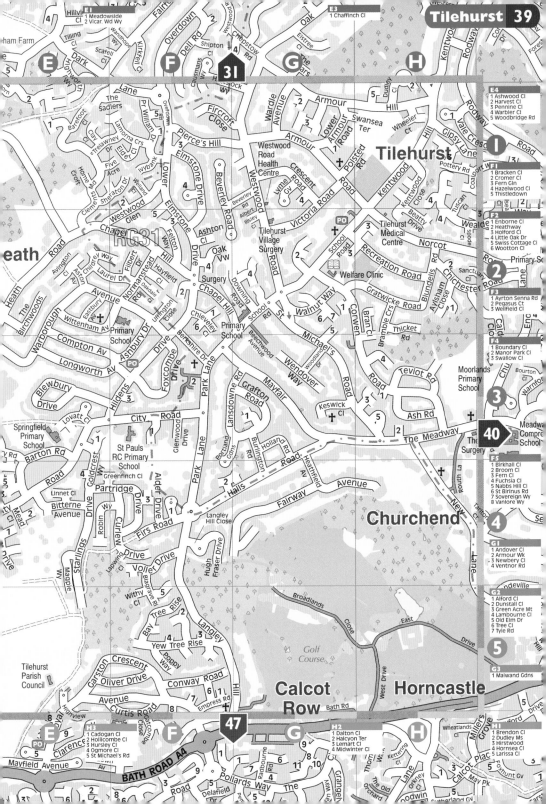

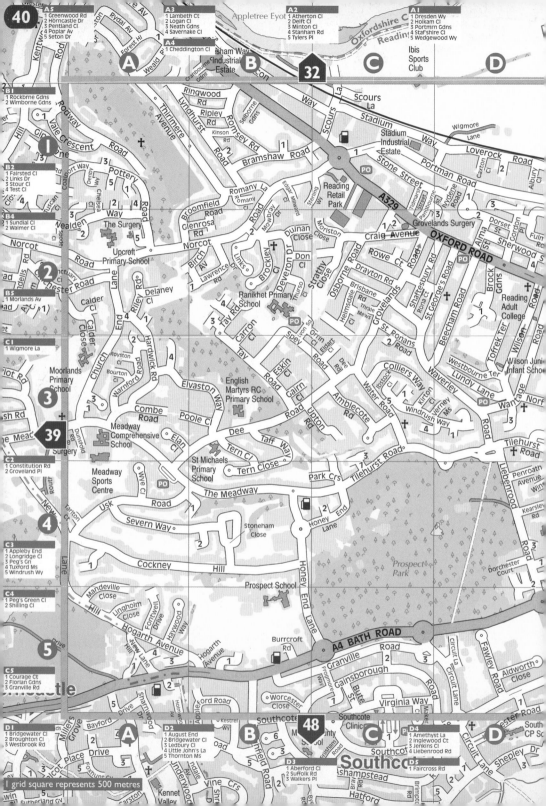

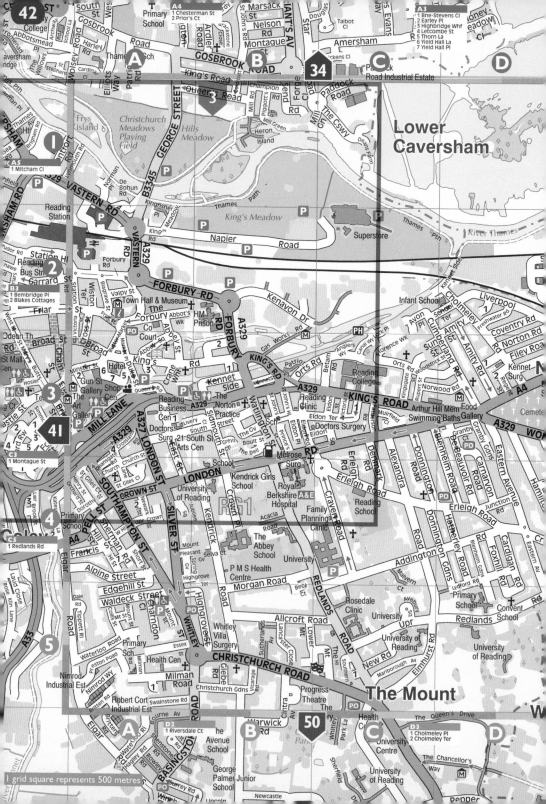

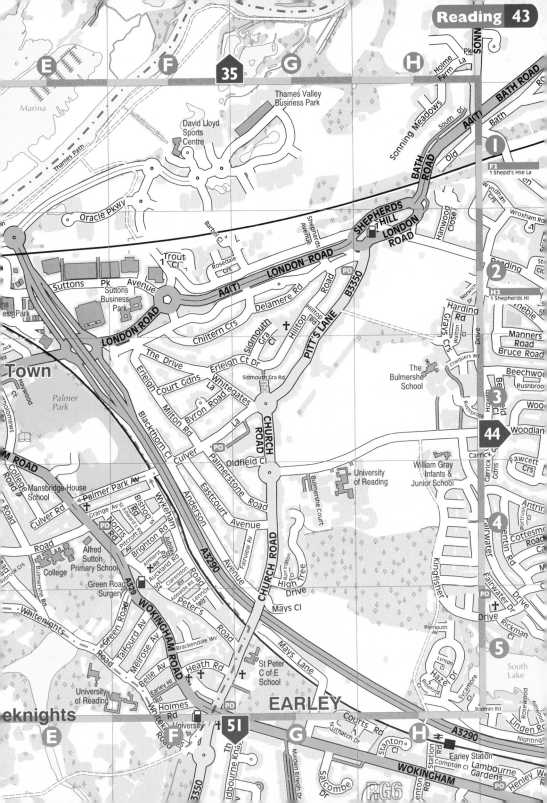

E
F
G
H

Landsend Lane

Whistley Mill Farm

37

Whistley Green

1 Lindberg Wy

B3030

A321

BROADWATER LANE

Hurst

River Loddon

LODGE ROAD

1 Buccaneer Cl
2 Constable Cl

St Nicholas C of E Primary School

Phillips Cl

Vulcan Close

Cody Cl
Marathon

Hurricane Wy

Master Cl

Blanchard Cl

Harris Cl

Anthan

Farman

Mollison Close

Harvard

Mohawk

Sandford Farm

Nursery Close

Barber Cl

Sawpit Rd

Sawpit Rd

Orchard Ro

Sunderland Cl

Woodley C of E Primary School

Walrus Cl

Church Hill

School

Rose Cl

Catalina Wy

New Way

Tiger Cl

Kittiwake

Beaver Cl

Mohawk

Hurst House

1 Martineau La

Sandford Lane

Colemans Moor Rd

Sandford Mill

M
The Museum of Berkshire Aviation

Hurst Grove

B3030

Lines Road

Sandford Lane

Hatch Gate Farm

Lines Road

Dinton Pastures

53

STREET

DAVIS

Douglas Grange

St Nicholas Farm

Dunt Lane

Dunt

Avenue

E
F
G
H

Monks Way
Winser Drive
Southcote Farm La
Killworth Avenue
Firs Lane
Edenham
Greenridge Ct
Rembrandt Way
Barrington
Primary School
Surgery
The Old La
Wensley Rd
Tintern Crs
Saviour's Road
Trelleck Road
Arbor Clos
Yew La
The Bro
The Old La
St
Wensley Road
Wensley Rd
Lesford Road
Heron Wy
Wensley Road

Rose Kiln Lane
River Kennet
A33

Nimrod Industrial Est
Nimrod Wy
Britten Rd
Elgar Rd
Preston Rd
Water Loo
Robert C Industrial

I
1 Cowper Wy

Cradock Road
Boulton Road
Arkwright Rd
Hagley

Rose Kiln La
Gillette Road

2
Hyperion Way
Superstore

The Micro Centre

Whitley

3
Manor Farm Rd

50

Commercial
Darwin Cl
Rd
Works
Works

A33
Smallmead Rd

4
B3031
BASINGSTOKE ROAD

Bennet Road

Works

Acre Road

Acre Business Park

Smallmead Road
Smallmead Road
Small Mead Farm

Reading
Wokingham

Hoops Wy
Royal Way
Shooters Wy
Boot End
Biscuit Wy
Hurst Way
Madejski Stadium

5
Hotel

Worton Dr
Worton Drive
BASINGSTOKE ROAD

Kennet and Avon Canal

Island Road

E
F
41
G
H

E
F
59
G
H

Imperial Way
A33
Heroes Wy

Reading Wokingham

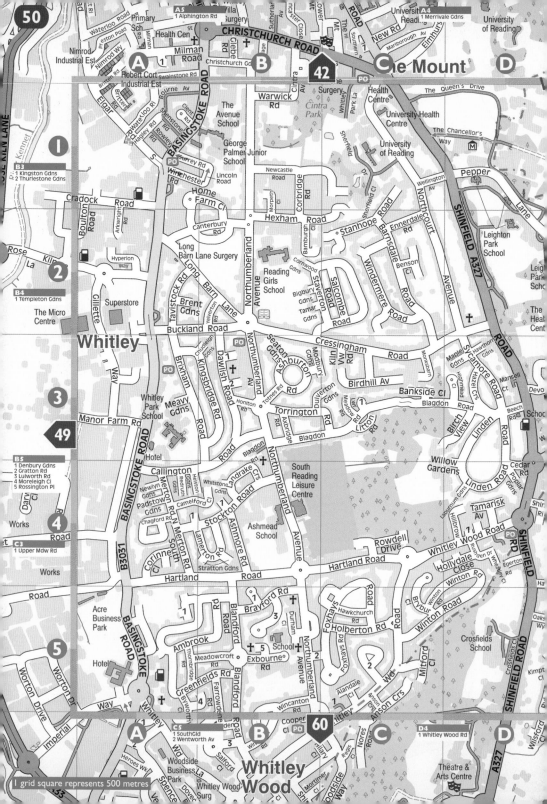

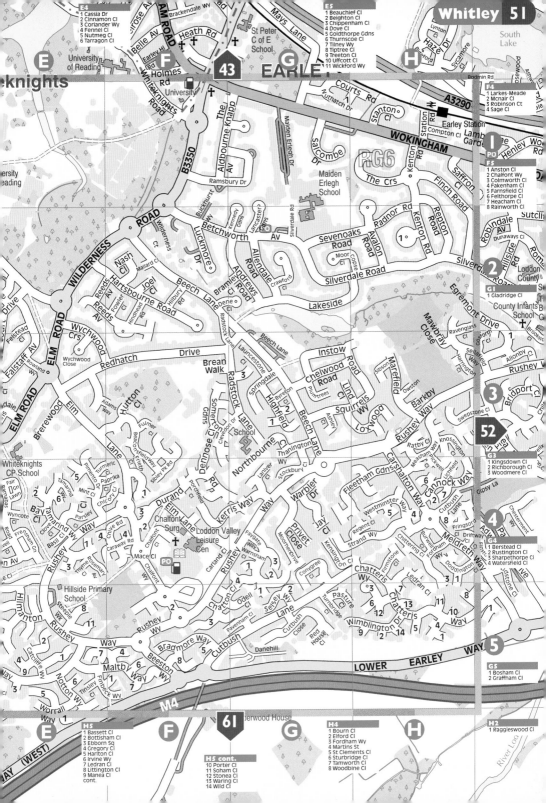

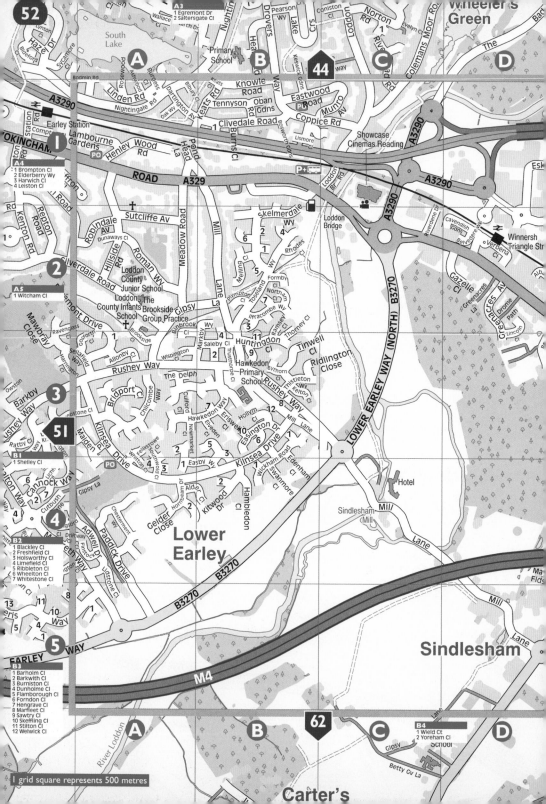

E4
1 Goddard Ct
2 Grasmere Cl
3 Wilson Ct

E3
1 Azalea Cl
2 Targett Ct

F2
1 The Priory
2 Windermere Cl

F3
1 Church Cl
2 Harefield Cl

G2
1 M'hill Grn La

G4
1 Sadler's Ct

G3
1 Alderney Gdns
2 Donnington Pl
3 Fieldway

Merryhill Green

Winnersh

The Forest Comprehensive School

Winnersh Station

Bearwood Primary School

Emmbrook

Hawthorns Primary

St Nic... Farm

Curtain Gallery

Sadlers

Roads and places:
Borrowdale Road, Arbor Mdw, Arbor Lane, Bluebell Meadow, Snowdrop Gv, Melody Close, Primrose La, Robin Hood Way, B3030, Sylvester Cl, Maple La, Meadow Vw, Poplar Lane, Greenwood, Groveland Cl, Astor Cl, Annesley Gdns, Sherwood Road, Deerhurst Av, Watmore La, Clarendon Cl, Birchmead, Danywern Drive, Garth Cl, Reynard Cl, Wedderburn La, Winnersh Gate, Eastbury Pk, Woodward, Woodward Cl, Pheasant La, Bathurst Road, Barlow Rd, Westfield Rd, Rainbow Pk, Harman Ct, Churchill Drive, Welby Crs, Russell Wy, Delane Dr, Bailey Ct, Eden Cl Way, King Street Lane, Sandstone, Alinatt Av, Dolphin Cl, Melbourne Av, Winnersh Rd, Laburnum Rd, Longdon Rd, Mermaid Cl, Dunst..., St Mary's Rd, B3030, Bearwood Road

Davis St, Davis Wy, Douglas Grange, Little Hill Road, Green Lane, Dunt Lane, Dunt Avenue, A329(M), M4, A329, Lenham Cl, Forest Rd, Sadler's La, Woodland Av, Reading Road, Simon's La, Roundabouts La, Walter Road, Windmill Av, Scots Dr, Camellia Way, Larkspur, Northway, Sapphire Cl, Quartz Cl, Foxglove, Bedford Gdns, Chestnut Avenue, Astley Cl, Old Wooseh... La, Lowther Rd, Lowther Cl, Lowther Road, Emmbrook Rd, Brimley, Bredon

PO

45
63

2
3
54
4
5

Junc...

Tou...

RD

E F G H I
E F G H

A
B
C
D

cholas Farm

Oakley Farm

Pound Lane

Nelso

Dunt Avenue

Lines Rd
Lines Road

A321

M4
Wa

1
Dunt

A 4
1 Beckford Cl
2 Woodhurst La

Lane

Dunt Lane

Bill Hill Park

2

A 5
1 Corfield Gn

Forest Road

B3034
FOREST

3

Junction 10

53
Toutley Industrial Estate

1
Toutley Industrial Estate

TWYFORD ROAD

B 3
1 Old Forest Rd

Toutley Road

Road

Ashton Rd

Summerfield Cl

Brimblecombe Close

A329(M)

4
Forest

Bredon Rd

Emley Close

7

Overbury Av

Toutley Cl

Commons Rd

Emmbrook Vale

Fullbrook Cl

Emmbrook County Junior & Infant School

Lowther Rd

Lowther Cl

1
Emmbrook Rd

2

Matthewsgreen

Sewell

Wokingham Theatre

Bell Foundry Lane

De

5

READING ROAD

Emmbrook Rd

Emm Cl

The Emmbrook School

Marks Road

Cantley Crs

Road

Deacon

Wiltshir

Emmbrook

PO

Bedford Gdns

Windmill Av

Valley Crs

Clifton

Brook

Avenue

A321

TWYFORD ROAD

Martins Drive

Jubil

Deacon

Bishops Rd

Dean Gv

Abbey Cl

dmill Av
Scots

Road

Chestnut Avenue

Woosehill La

Astley Cl

estwood Rd

Mill

Millmead

Rotherfield Av

Copse Dr

64
Matthewsgreen

venue

Larch Av

MILTON RO

Tamarisk Rise

Deacon Rd

Acon

A
B
C
D

I grid square represents 500 metres

Primary School

2

A329

Lane

The Holt School

kwart

Drive

E F Windsor and Maidenhead G H

Wokingham

Straight Mile Farm

The Straight Mile

Carter's Hill

I

Maidenhead Road

Marchfield House

2

ROAD

Green Lane

BIN

3

Roughgr
Copse

Ashridge Manor

Kingscote

Warren House Road

Rushton's Farm

Binfield Road

Bracknell Forest
Wokingham

4

ES
1 Headington Cl

5

esgreen

Warren House Rd

Green Croft

Pigott

Stokes Farm

Ashridge Rd

Eustace Crescent

Moores Geen

Hutsons Cl

Rosebay

Webb Ct

Macphail Cl

Blake Cl

Whaley Rd

Child

Sorrel Cl

Payley Drive

Comfrey Cl

Montague Close

Budge's Road

Keephatch Rd

Sundew Cl

Trefoil Cl

Clover Cl

Monkshood Cl

Willowhe

Keep Hatch

65

E Burma Hills Surgery F G H

Palace Gn

rum Crs

ngton

Ward Cl

nesfield Crs

Leney Way

Sherfield

Avenue Infants School

Keep Hatch County Junior School

Hughes Rd

Twycross Road

Dyer Rd

Patten

Long

Binfield Road

A329(M)

3

E

F

49

G

H

Madjeski Stadium

Royal

Wy

Boot End

Biscuit Wy

Hurst Way

Worton Dr

Worton Drive

Imperial

Way

Hotel

I

Heroes Wk

Kingsley Cl

A33

Whitley

Reading Wokingham

M4

Hartley Court

Kybes Lane

Hartley

Court

Road

Hopkiln Farm

Berkshire

Wokingham

Great Lea

Great Lea Common

2

Junctio

BASINGSTOKE ROAD

Mereoak Lane

Great Lea

Basingstoke Road

3

60

Basingstoke Road

PO

Churc

Three Mile Cr

4

Grazeley

Road

Woodcock Ct

eley Court Farm

Mereoak Lane

Mereoak Lane

A33

Sevenoaks Dr

Stanbury Park

5

Halfacre Cl

Askew Clo

Recreation

The Sq

La

Orc

ndgreen

Bloomfieldhatch Lane

E

F

G

H

†

Grazeley

Grazeley School

Spencers Wood

LOWER EARLEY

E

F
M4

51

G

H

Upperwood House

I

E1
1 Tickhill Cl

WAY (WEST)

Curbush Lane

Shinfield
Grange

RG2

2

E4
1 Wickers Cl

River Loddon

Hall Farm

3

62

4

Church

School

Parrot Farm

ARBORFIELD ROAD   A327

Arborfield

Church La

hinfield
of E
unior School

Bridge Farm

READING

ROAD

Walden Av

5

Ar
Cro

E

F

67

G

Greensward

H

Lane

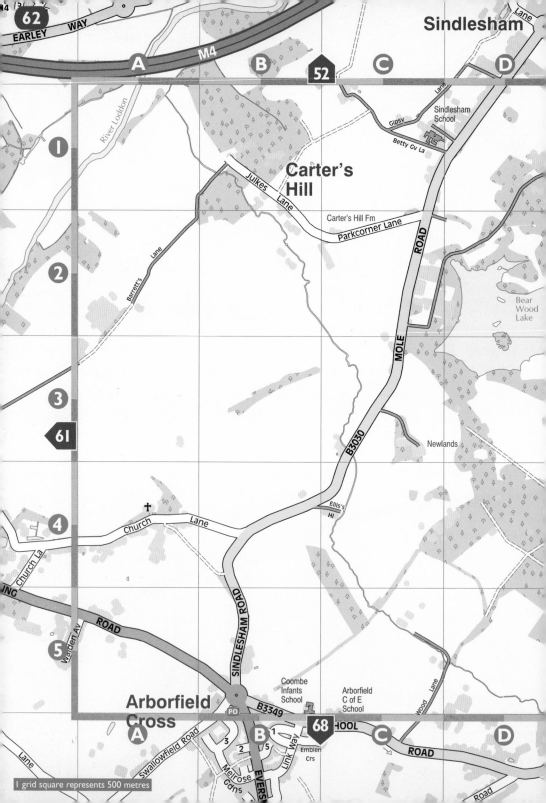

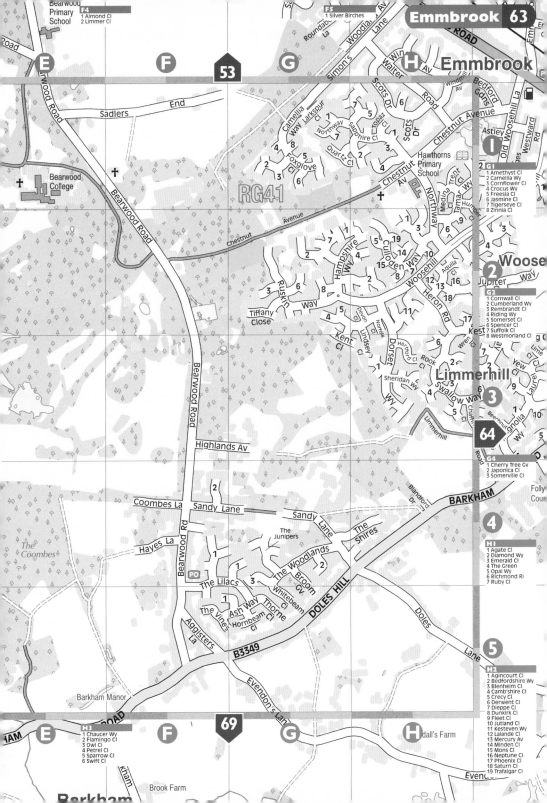

Bearwood
Primary
School

F4
1 Almond Cl
2 Limmer Cl

F5
1 Silver Birches

E **F** **53** **G** **H** Emmbrook

ROAD

Sadlers End

Inwood Road

Bearwood
College

RG41

Bearwood Road

Chestnut Avenue

Simon's

Woodland La

Roundabout La

Woodland Lane

Win
Walter
Road

Scots Dr

Scots Dr

Camellia Way

Larkspur
Northway

Foxglove

Quartz Cl

Sapphire Cl

Chestnut Av

Northway

Hawthorns
Primary
School

Windmill

Bedford Gdns

Old Woosehill La

Astley

Westward Rd

I

G1
1 Amethyst Cl
2 Camellia Wy
3 Cornflower Cl
4 Crocus Wy
5 Freesia Cl
6 Jasmine Cl
7 Tigerseye Cl
8 Zinnia Cl

Chestnut Avenue

Ruskin Way

Tiffany Close

Hampshire Wy

Culloden Way

Woosehill

Heron Rd

Medni

Trent

Tamar

Humber

Aquila

Jupiter Way

2 Woose

G2
1 Cornwall Cl
2 Cumberland Wy
3 Rembrandt Cl
4 Riding Wy
5 Somerset Cl
6 Spencer Cl
7 Suffolk Cl
8 Westmorland Cl

Kent Cl

Lindsey

Dorset

Devon

Norfolk

Hertford Dr

Rook

Sheridan Wy

Swallow Way

Chatham

Wren

Kesten

Yew

Laurel

Lime

Limmerhill

Limmerhill

Beech

Magnolia

3

64

G4
1 Cherry Tree Gv
2 Japonica Cl
3 Somerville Cl

Highlands Av

Coombes La

Sandy Lane

Bearwood Rd

Sandy Lane

The Junipers

The Shires

Blandford Dr

BARKHAM

4

H1
1 Agate Cl
2 Diamond Wy
3 Emerald Cl
4 The Green
5 Opal Wy
6 Richmond Ri
7 Ruby Cl

The Coombes

Hayes La

PO

The Lilacs

The Vines

Ash Way

Hornbeam Cl

Whitebeam

Thorne

The Woodlands

Broom Gv

DOLES HILL

Doles Lane

5

H2
1 Agincourt Cl
2 Bedfordshire Wy
3 Blenheim Cl
4 Camb'shire Cl
5 Crecy Cl
6 Derwent Cl
7 Dieppe Cl
8 Dunkirk Cl
9 Fleet Cl
10 Jutland Cl
11 Kesteven Wy
12 Lalande Cl
13 Mercury Av
14 Minden Cl
15 Mons Cl
16 Neptune Cl
17 Phoenix Cl
18 Saturn Cl
19 Trafalgar Cl

Aggisters La

B3349

Barkham Manor

Evendon's Lan

E **H3**
1 Chaucer Wy
2 Flamingo Cl
3 Owl Cl
4 Petrel Cl
5 Sparrow Cl
6 Swift Cl
F **69** **G** **H** dall's Farm

Barkham

Brook Farm

Evendon

E F **61** G H

Arb
Cr

Greensward Lane

Swa

1

Arborfield Co

Swallowfield Road

2

White's Farm

Nurter's

Lane

Great
Wood

Tanner's Farm

Swallowfield Road

3

68

Moor
Copse

Swallowfield Road

Castle Hill

4

The
Chatters

Parsons Farm

Kiln Hill

Swallowfield Road

Road

5

ch

Lane

PH

Swallowfield

Rowe's Farm

Bungler's Hill

metery

E F G H

✝

Farley
Court

Farley Hill
Primary
School

F

Arborfield Cross

Coombe Infants School

Arborfield C of E School

62

SCHOOL ROAD

B3349

PO

Swallowfield Road

Melrose Gdns

Link Way

Emblen Crs

EVERSLEY ROAD

A327

B1
1 Anderson Crs
2 Brants Cl
3 Chambn's Gdns
4 Harts Cl
5 Whitewell Cl

Swallowfield Road

Lane

Arborfield Court

B4
1 Faraday Cl
2 Kelvin Cl

67

Rickman Cl

Langley

Common Road

Langley Com

Prs Marina Dr

Princess

Hilborn Way

James Watt Rd

Faraday Wy

College

REME Museum

Hill Rd

Valon Road

Venning Rd

Venning Rd

Biggs La

Biggs Lane

Isaac Newton Rd

Buttenshaw Avenue

Buttenshaw Cl

Bramshill Close

Baird Road

Whitehall Dr

EVERSLEY ROAD

Baird

Fleming Cl

Tyler Dr

Barker Cl

Sheerlands

Rowcroft Rd

Prs Marina Dr

Tope Rd

Parsons Rd

Stephenson Rd

Arborfield Garrison

Princess Marina Drive

Nuffield Road

Road

Whitworth Rd

Parsons Farm

Church Lane

Westwood Farm

Sheerlands Road

James Watt Road

Weller Dr

Marino Way

Ivanhoe Road

Hogw... La

Hogwood Farm

Farley Hill

Primary School

I grid square represents 500 metres

B3349

E
Barkham Manor

F

63
Evendon's Lane

G

H

ROAD

Barkham Street

Brook Farm

Randall's Farm

Redlands Pl

Evendon's Lane

I

G4
1 Fernbank
2 Oregon Wk

Barkham

Waverley
School

Church La

Barkham
Square

Commonfield Lane

Drive

Park Lane

Barkham Ride

Gilbert
Way

Booth Dr

Nash Grove

Waverley Way

2

G5
1 Manor Park Dr

Springdale

Thomas La

The Lea

1

2

4

The Spinney

Mc Carthy

The Mor

Garrett Rd

St James Road

Roycroft Lane

Ditchfield La

3

5

70

Nash

H2
1 Goldsmith Cl

Radical La

Maryland

Barkham Ride

Moor Cl

Gorse Ride N

Drake Cl

Barkham Rid

Vermont
Woods

Carolina Pl

3

1

Arne

4

H3
1 Fir Cottage Rd
2 Woodside Cl

2

4

Chivers
Dr

Gorse Ride S

Buchanan Dr

Whittle

Firs

Darc Cl

Av

2

Long
Moor

California Country
Park

Coleshill Farm

Wimbushes

Wimbushes

Hazelbank

Church
Rams

Gibbs Cl

Kelsey Av

Orbit

Billing Av

PO

1

2

3

5

FINCHAMPSTEAD ROAD

Nine Mile Ride

Warren

Lane

E

H5
1 Briarwood Dr
2 Manor Park Dr
3 Redgauntlet

F

White Horse Lane

G

H4
1 Chivers Dr
2 Columbia Ct
3 Copse Wy
4 Heather Cl

H

Warren
Lodge

Gorse Ride
Junior
School

Holme Green

E **F** **G** **H**

65

Heathlands

Easthampstead Rd

Holme Grange School

Lane

Redlake

M Old Art Gallery

Easthampstead Road

Gardeners Green

Sutton Court Farm

I

Honey Hill

Heathlands Road

Honey Hill

2

Honey Hill

Hatch Ride

3

St Sebastians Primary School

Heathlands

St Sebastian's Cl

Grove Cl

MILE RIDE B3430

Palmer Cl

Carnation Cl

Royal Oak Dr

Queens Ride

G5
1 Green Finch Cl

NINE

Holmbury Av

The Conifers

Honeysuckle Cl

Fern Cl

Brackens

Hatch Ride Primary School

4

H4
1 Edgewood Cl
2 Sweetbriar
3 Thorne Cl

Soldiers Rise

Heath Lake

Oleander Close

Greenfield

Otter Cl

Marigold Close

Wentworth Wy

Merryman Drive

St Andrews

Haybrook

Holme

The Leith Cl

Eagle Cl

New Wokingham Road

Oaklands La

Keats Av

Elgar Av

Purcell

New Wokingham Rd

Greenwood Rd

Butler

Grange Av

Eve

Hilary Drive

5

Ravenswood Village Settlement

LOWER

The Brambles

Bramley Gv

WOKINGHAM

Heathermount Drive

The Chase

Bramblegate

The Paddock

Birch Side

Edcumbe Park Drive

Greenside

Heatherway

Highway

Oakland County Junior & Infant School

Ellis

Corsham Wy

West Dunford Drive

Wiltshire Avenue

Aldworth Gdns

Preparatory School

The Avenue

Lynch

Thornbury

The Surgery

E **F** **G** **H**

East Berkshire Golf Club

The Devil's Hwy

Wellesley

Ride

Linkway

Parkway

Dormer

Arborfield	61 G4	Embmook	53 H5
Arborfield Cross	62 A5	Emmer Green	33 H1
Arborfield Garrison	68 D4	Exlade Street	11 E1
Aston	7 F1	Gallowstree Common	12 B4
Barkham	69 E1	Gardeners Green	71 E1
Binfield Heath	25 F3	Goring	8 B3
Borough Marsh	26 D4	Goring Heath	20 D1
Broadplat	4 D2	Grazeley Green	58 A5
Burghfield	57 F3	Great Lea Common	59 H2
Burghfield Hill	57 F5	Greys Green	4 C4
Calcot	47 F1	Harpsden	16 B3
Calcot Row	39 G5	Harpsden Bottom	15 G3
Cane End	22 A1	Heathlands	71 G3
Carter's Hill	62 B1	Henley-on-Thames	6 A5
Caversham	33 G4	Hill Bottom	20 B1
Caversham Heights	33 G3	Holme Green	65 G5
Chalkhouse Green	23 H3	Honey Hill	71 H2
Charvil	36 D2	Hook End	11 G1
Chazey Heath	22 D5	Horncastle	39 H5
Churchend	39 H4	Kidmore End	22 D1
Cleeve	8 B1	Langley Common	68 C2
Cold Harbour	9 G5	Limmerhill	63 H3
Coley	41 H4	Little Heath	38 D2
Collins End	21 E2	Littlestead Green	34 D1
Cray's Pond	10 A3	Lower Basildon	18 C2
Crazies Hill	17 H3	Lower Caversham	42 C1
Cross Lanes	21 H3	Lower Earley	52 A4
Crowsley	14 B5	Lower Shiplake	26 C1
Dowlesgreen	54 D5	Malpas	38 A4
Dunsden Green	25 E5	Mapledurham	31 H1
Earley	43 G5	Matthewsgreen	64 B1
Eastheath	64 B5	Mays Green	15 G4
Merryhill Green	53 G2	Sulham	38 B1
The Mount	42 C5	Sulhampstead Abbots	56 C4
New Cross	26 B2	Sulhampstead	
Newtown	16 B1	Bannister Upper End	56 A3
New Town	28 B3	Swallowfield	66 C5
New Town	42 D3	Theale	46 A2
North Street	38 A5	Three Mile Cross	60 A4
Nuney Green	21 H1	The Throat	70 B2
Pangbourne	29 G2	Tidmarsh	29 G5
Pingewood	48 D5	Tilehurst	39 H1
Play Hatch	35 E2	Tokers Green	23 E5
Poundgreen	58 D5	Trash Green	56 D1
Purley on Thames	30 D3	Trench Green	22 B5
Ravenswood Village Settlement	71 F5	Twyford	37 H2
Reading	2 E5	Ufton Nervet	56 A4
Remenham	6 C1	Wargrave	27 F3
Remenham Hill	7 F4	Wheeler's Green	44 D5
Rotherfield Greys	4 B5	Whistley Green	45 H1
Rotherfield Peppard	13 G2	Whitchurch Hill	20 B2
Ruscombe	37 H2	Whitchurch-on-Thames	19 G5
Ryeish Green	60 B4	Whitehouse Green	56 D2
Schoolgreen	60 C4	Whiteknights	50 D1
Sheffield Bottom	46 C5	Whitley	49 H3
Shinfield	60 C3	Whitley Wood	60 B1
Shiplake	26 B2	Wick Hill	70 B5
Shiplake Bottom	13 F3	Winnersh	53 E3
Shiplake Row	25 C2	Wokingham	65 E2
Sindlesham	52 C5	Woodcote	10 B1
Sonning	36 A3	Woodlands	6 B4
Sonning Common	13 F3	Woodley	44 C4
Sonning Eye	35 H2	Woodley Green	44 C3
Southcote	48 C1	Woose Hill	64 A2

USING THE STREET INDEX

Street names are listed alphabetically. Each street name is followed by its postal town or area locality, the Postcode District, the page number, and the reference to the square in which the name is found.

Abbots Cl *GOR/PANG* RG8 .... 10 C1 🔟

Some entries are followed by a number in a blue box. This number indicates the location of the street within the referenced grid square. The full street name is listed at the side of the map page.

GENERAL ABBREVIATIONS

ACC	ACCESS	CYN	CANYON	HTS	HEIGHTS	PAS	PASSAGE
ALY	ALLEY	DEPT	DEPARTMENT	HVN	HAVEN	PAV	PAVILION
AP	APPROACH	DL	DALE	HWY	HIGHWAY	PDE	PARADE
AR	ARCADE	DM	DAM	IMP	IMPERIAL	PH	PUBLIC HOUSE
ASS	ASSOCIATION	DR	DRIVE	IN	INLET	PK	PARK
AV	AVENUE	DRO	DROVE	IND EST	INDUSTRIAL ESTATE	PKWY	PARKWAY
BCH	BEACH	DRY	DRIVEWAY	INF	INFIRMARY	PL	PLACE
BLDS	BUILDINGS	DWGS	DWELLINGS	INFO	INFORMATION	PLN	PLAIN
BND	BEND	E	EAST	INT	INTERCHANGE	PLNS	PLAINS
BNK	BANK	EMB	EMBANKMENT	IS	ISLAND	PLZ	PLAZA
BR	BRIDGE	EMBY	EMBASSY	JCT	JUNCTION	POL	POLICE STATION
BRK	BROOK	ESP	ESPLANADE	JTY	JETTY	PR	PRINCE
BTM	BOTTOM	EST	ESTATE	KG	KING	PREC	PRECINCT
BUS	BUSINESS	EX	EXCHANGE	KNL	KNOLL	PREP	PREPARATORY
BVD	BOULEVARD	EXPY	EXPRESSWAY	L	LAKE	PRIM	PRIMARY
BY	BYPASS	EXT	EXTENSION	LA	LANE	PROM	PROMENADE
CATH	CATHEDRAL	F/O	FLYOVER	LDG	LODGE	PRS	PRINCESS
CEM	CEMETERY	FC	FOOTBALL CLUB	LGT	LIGHT	PRT	PORT
CEN	CENTRE	FK	FORK	LK	LOCK	PT	POINT
CFT	CROFT	FLD	FIELD	LKS	LAKES	PTH	PATH
CH	CHURCH	FLDS	FIELDS	LNDG	LANDING	PZ	PIAZZA
CHA	CHASE	FLS	FALLS	LTL	LITTLE	QD	QUADRANT
CHYD	CHURCHYARD	FLS	FLATS	LWR	LOWER	QU	QUEEN
CIR	CIRCLE	FM	FARM	MAG	MAGISTRATE	QY	QUAY
CIRC	CIRCUS	FT	FORT	MAN	MANSIONS	R	RIVER
CL	CLOSE	FWY	FREEWAY	MD	MEAD	RBT	ROUNDABOUT
CLFS	CLIFFS	FY	FERRY	MDW	MEADOWS	RD	ROAD
CMP	CAMP	GA	GATE	MEM	MEMORIAL	RDG	RIDGE
CNR	CORNER	GAL	GALLERY	MKT	MARKET	REP	REPUBLIC
CO	COUNTY	GDN	GARDEN	MKTS	MARKETS	RES	RESERVOIR
COLL	COLLEGE	GDNS	GARDENS	ML	MALL	RFC	RUGBY FOOTBALL CLUB
COM	COMMON	GLD	GLADE	ML	MILL	RI	RISE
COMM	COMMISSION	GLN	GLEN	MNR	MANOR	RP	RAMP
CON	CONVENT	GN	GREEN	MS	MEWS	RW	ROW
COT	COTTAGE	GND	GROUND	MSN	MISSION	S	SOUTH
COTS	COTTAGES	GRA	GRANGE	MT	MOUNT	SCH	SCHOOL
CP	CAPE	GRG	GARAGE	MTN	MOUNTAIN	SE	SOUTH EAST
CPS	COPSE	GT	GREAT	MTS	MOUNTAINS	SER	SERVICE AREA
CR	CREEK	GTWY	GATEWAY	MUS	MUSEUM	SH	SHORE
CREM	CREMATORIUM	GV	GROVE	MWY	MOTORWAY	SHOP	SHOPPING
CRS	CRESCENT	HGR	HIGHER	N	NORTH	SKWY	SKYWAY
CSWY	CAUSEWAY	HL	HILL	NE	NORTH EAST	SMT	SUMMIT
CT	COURT	HLS	HILLS	NW	NORTH WEST	SOC	SOCIETY
CTRL	CENTRAL	HO	HOUSE	O/P	OVERPASS	SP	SPUR
CTS	COURTS	HOL	HOLLOW	OFF	OFFICE	SPR	SPRING
CTYD	COURTYARD	HOSP	HOSPITAL	ORCH	ORCHARD	SQ	SQUARE
CUTT	CUTTINGS	HRB	HARBOUR	OV	OVAL	ST	STREET
CV	COVE	HTH	HEATH	PAL	PALACE	STN	STATION

STR	STREAM	TR	TRACK

STR ....STREAM
STRD ....STRAND
SW ....SOUTH WEST
TDG ....TRADING
TER ....TERRACE
THWY ....THROUGHWAY
TNL ....TUNNEL
TOLL ....TOLLWAY
TPK ....TURNPIKE

TR ....TRACK
TRL ....TRAIL
TWR ....TOWER
U/P ....UNDERPASS
UNI ....UNIVERSITY
UPR ....UPPER
V ....VALE
VA ....VALLEY
VIAD ....VIADUCT

VIL ....VILLA
VIS ....VISTA
VLG ....VILLAGE
VLS ....VILLAS
VW ....VIEW
W ....WEST
WD ....WOOD
WHF ....WHARF
WK ....WALK

WKS ....WALKS
WLS ....WELLS
WY ....WAY
YD ....YARD
YHA ....YOUTH HOSTEL

POSTCODE TOWNS AND AREA ABBREVIATIONS

BNFD ....Binfield
CAV/SC ....Caversham/Sonning Common
CWTH ....Crowthorne
EARL ....Earley

EWKG ....Wokingham east
GOR/PANG ....Goring/Pangbourne
HEN ....Henley-on-Thames
MLW ....Marlow

RDGW ....Reading West
READ ....Reading
THLE ....Theale
TLHT ....Tilehurst

WAR/TWY ....Wargrave/Twyford
WHIT ....Whitley/Arborfield
WODY ....Woodley
WWKG ....Wokingham west

Index - streets

Aba - Bel

A

Abattoirs Rd READ RG1 .... 2 D3
Abbey Cl EWKG RG40 .... 64 D1
Abbey Pk THLE RG7 .... 56 C5
Abbey Sq READ RG1 .... 3 G5
Abbey St READ RG1 .... 3 G5
Abbots Cl GOR/PANG RG8 .... 10 C1
Abbotsmead Pl READ RG1 .... 33 H5
Abbot's Rd THLE RG7 .... 56 C5
Abbot's Wk READ RG1 .... 3 G4
Aberaman CAV/SC RG4 .... 33 G1
Aberford Cl RDGW RG30 .... 40 D3
Abingdon Dr CAV/SC RG4 .... 34 B1
Abrahams Rd HEN RG9 .... 5 H3
Acorn Dr EWKG RG40 .... 64 D1
Acre Rd WHIT RG2 .... 49 H5
Adam Ct HEN RG9 .... 6 A4
Adams Wy EARL RG6 .... 51 E3
Addington Rd READ RG1 .... 42 C4
Addiscombe Cha CALC RG31 .... 31 E4
Addison Rd EARL RG6 .... 43 F5
Adelaide Rd EARL RG6 .... 43 F5
Admirals Ct WHIT RG2 .... 41 H4
Adwell Dr EARL RG6 .... 52 A4
Adwell Sq HEN RG9 .... 6 A4
Agate Cl WWKG RG41 .... 63 H1
Aggisters La WWKG RG41 .... 63 F5
Agincourt La WWKG RG41 .... 63 H2
Ainsdale Crs RDGW RG30 .... 48 B1
Alandale Cl WHIT RG2 .... 50 C5
Albany Park Dr WWKG RG41 .... 52 D2
Albany Rd RDGW RG30 .... 41 E3
Albert Illsley Cl CALC RG31 .... 39 G2
Albert Rd EARL RG6 .... 43 G3
EWKG RG40 .... 64 C3
HEN RG9 .... 6 B5
Albury Cl RDGW RG30 .... 40 D1
Albury Gdns CALC RG31 .... 47 H2
Aldbourne Av EARL RG6 .... 51 F1
Aldeburgh Cl CAV/SC RG4 .... 24 B4
Aldenham Cl CAV/SC RG4 .... 34 B1
Alder Cl EARL RG6 .... 52 A4
Alder Dr CALC RG31 .... 39 F4
Alderfield Cl THLE RG7 .... 46 C1
Alder Gld THLE RG7 .... 56 C5
Alderley Rd WODY RG5 .... 44 C1
Alderman Willey Cl
EWKG RG40 .... 64 C2
Alderney Gdns WWKG RG41 .... 53 G3
Aldworth Cl RDGW RG30 .... 40 D5
Aldeburgh Cl CAV/SC RG4 .... 24 B4
Aldenham Cl CAV/SC RG4 .... 34 B1
Alexandra Ct EWKG RG40 .... 64 D3
Alexandra Rd READ RG1 .... 42 C3
Alford Cl RDGW RG30 .... 39 G2
Alfred St READ RG1 .... 2 C5
Allcroft Rd READ RG1 .... 42 B5
Allendale Rd EARL RG6 .... 51 G2
All Hallows Rd CAV/SC RG4 .... 34 C4
Allison Gdns GOR/PANG RG8 .... 31 F2
Allnatt Av WWKG RG41 .... 53 F4
Allonby Rd EARL RG6 .... 52 A3
All Saints Cl EWKG RG40 .... 64 D1
Alma St RDGW RG30 .... 40 D2
Almond Cl WWKG RG41 .... 63 H4
Almond Dr CAV/SC RG4 .... 35 E3
Alphington Rd WHIT RG2 .... 50 A5
Alpine St READ RG1 .... 42 A4
Amberley Dr WAR/TWY RG10 .... 37 G1
Amblecote Dr RDGW RG30 .... 40 C3
Ambleside Cl WODY RG5 .... 44 B3
Ambrook Rd WHIT RG2 .... 50 A5
Ambrose Pl READ RG1 .... 2 C5
Amersham Rd CAV/SC RG4 .... 34 C5

Amethyst Cl WWKG RG41 .... 63 G1
Amethyst La RDGW RG30 .... 40 D4
Amherst Rd EARL RG6 .... 43 F4
Amity Rd READ RG1 .... 42 D3
Amity St READ RG1 .... 42 D3
Ammanford Av CAV/SC RG4 .... 33 G2
Amners Farm Rd RDGW RG30 .... 48 A5
Ancastle Gn HEN RG9 .... 5 H5
Anderson Av EARL RG6 .... 43 F4
Anderson Crs WHIT RG2 .... 68 B1
Andover Cl CALC RG31 .... 39 G1
Andrew Cl EWKG RG40 .... 65 F3
Andrews Cl THLE RG7 .... 46 B2
Andrews Rd EARL RG6 .... 51 G2
Angle Field Rd CAV/SC RG4 .... 34 B4
Anglers Wy READ RG1 .... 3 K5
Angus Cl CALC RG31 .... 47 H1
Annesley Gdns WWKG RG41 .... 53 F2
Anson Crs WHIT RG2 .... 60 C1
Anstey Pl THLE RG7 .... 56 D5
Anstey Rd READ RG1 .... 2 D6
Anston Cl EARL RG6 .... 51 F5
Antares Cl WWKG RG41 .... 64 A2
Anthian Cl WODY RG5 .... 45 E2
Antrim Rd WODY RG5 .... 44 A4
Appleby End RDGW RG30 .... 40 C3
Apple Cl CALC RG31 .... 31 E3
WWKG RG41 .... 64 A3
Appleford Rd RDGW RG30 .... 48 B1
Appletree Cl CAV/SC RG4 .... 13 F3
Appletree La THLE RG7 .... 66 A1
Aquila Cl WWKG RG41 .... 63 H2
Arborfield Rd WHIT RG2 .... 61 E4
Arbor La WWKG RG41 .... 53 E2
Arbor Mdw WWKG RG41 .... 53 E2
Arbour Cl READ RG1 .... 41 G5
Archway Rd READ RG1 .... 33 H5
Ardler Rd CAV/SC RG4 .... 34 B5
Argyle Cl WHIT RG2 .... 2 A1
Argyle St READ RG1 .... 2 A5
Arkwright Rd WHIT RG2 .... 50 A2
Armadale Ct RDGW RG30 .... 41 E4
Armour Hl CALC RG31 .... 39 G1
Armour Rd CALC RG31 .... 39 G1
Armour Wk CALC RG31 .... 39 G1
Armstrong Wy WODY RG5 .... 44 D3
Arnett Av EWKG RG40 .... 69 H4
Arnside Rd WAR/TWY RG10 .... 27 G2
Arrowhead Rd THLE RG7 .... 46 C3
Arthur Rd WWKG RG41 .... 64 B1
Arun Cl WWKG RG41 .... 53 E4
Arundel Rd WODY RG5 .... 44 B4
Ashampstead Rd RDGW RG30 .... 48 C1
Ashburton Rd WHIT RG2 .... 50 B3
Ashbury Dr CALC RG31 .... 39 E5
Ashby Ct WHIT RG2 .... 60 A1
Ashcroft Cl CAV/SC RG4 .... 33 F2
Ashdale Pk EWKG RG40 .... 70 A4
Ashford Av CAV/SC RG4 .... 13 F4
Ash La THLE RG7 .... 56 D4
Ashlee Wk GOR/PANG RG8 .... 10 C1
Ashley Cl EARL RG6 .... 51 G3
Ashley Rd READ RG1 .... 41 F4
Ashmere Cl CALC RG31 .... 47 F1
Ashmere Ter RDGW RG30 .... 41 F2
Ashmore Rd WHIT RG2 .... 50 B4
Ashridge Rd EWKG RG40 .... 55 E5
Ash Rd RDGW RG30 .... 39 H3
Ashton Cl CALC RG31 .... 39 F2
Ashton Rd WHIT RG2 .... 54 A4
Ashtrees Rd WODY RG5 .... 44 C2
Ashville Wy WWKG RG41 .... 64 B3
Ash Wy WWKG RG41 .... 63 G5
Ashwood WODY RG5 .... 44 A5
Ashwood Cl CALC RG31 .... 39 E4

Askew Dr THLE RG7 .... 60 A5
Astley Cl WWKG RG41 .... 64 A1
Aston Av CALC RG31 .... 39 E2
Aston Cl GOR/PANG RG8 .... 30 A2
Aston Ferry La HEN RG9 .... 7 F1
Aston La HEN RG9 .... 7 F3
Astor Cl WWKG RG41 .... 53 G2
Atherton Cl RDGW RG30 .... 40 A2
Auckland Rd EARL RG6 .... 43 F4
Audley St RDGW RG30 .... 41 E2
August End RDGW RG30 .... 40 D3
Austin Rd WODY RG5 .... 44 C4
Auton Pl HEN RG9 .... 16 A1
Autumn Cl CAV/SC RG4 .... 24 B5
Autumn Wk WAR/TWY RG10 .... 27 G2
Avalon Rd EARL RG6 .... 51 H2
Avebury Sq READ RG1 .... 42 C4
Avery Cl EWKG RG40 .... 70 A5
Avington Cl CALC RG31 .... 39 E2
Avon Pl READ RG1 .... 42 C2
Axbridge Rd WHIT RG2 .... 50 B3
Aylsham Cl RDGW RG30 .... 39 H2
Ayrton Senna Rd CALC RG31 .... 39 F3
Azalea Cl WWKG RG41 .... 53 E3

B

Babbington Rd WHIT RG2 .... 60 C2
Backsideans WAR/TWY RG10 .... 27 G2
The Bader Wy WODY RG5 .... 44 D5
Badgemore La HEN RG9 .... 6 A3
Badger Dr WAR/TWY RG10 .... 27 G5
Badgers Ri CAV/SC RG4 .... 33 H2
Badgers Wk HEN RG9 .... 26 D1
Bainbridge Rd CALC RG31 .... 39 E5
Baird Rd WHIT RG2 .... 68 B3
Baker St READ RG1 .... 2 B6
Baldons Cl GOR/PANG RG8 .... 10 C1
Balfour Dr CALC RG31 .... 47 E1
Ballamoor Cl CALC RG31 .... 46 D1
Balliol Rd CAV/SC RG4 .... 33 E4
Balme Cl WAR/TWY RG10 .... 37 E4
Balmore Dr CAV/SC RG4 .... 34 A3
Balmore Pk CAV/SC RG4 .... 33 H3
Bamburgh Cl WHIT RG2 .... 50 B2
Bamford Pl CALC RG31 .... 47 E1
Banbury Gdns CAV/SC RG4 .... 34 B4
Bancroft Pl CALC RG31 .... 47 E2
Bank Side EWKG RG40 .... 70 A5
Bankside Cl WHIT RG2 .... 50 C3
Barbara's Meadow CALC RG31 .... 31 E5
Barbel Cl EARL RG6 .... 43 F2
Barber Cl WAR/TWY RG10 .... 37 E4
Barbrook Cl CALC RG31 .... 31 G4
Barclay Rd CALC RG31 .... 47 F2
Barclose Av CAV/SC RG4 .... 34 B4
Bardolph's Cl CAV/SC RG4 .... 23 E4
Barefoot Cl EARL RG6 .... 51 E1
Barholm Cl EARL RG6 .... 52 B3
Barkby EARL RG6 .... 51 H3
Barker Cl WHIT RG2 .... 68 B4
Barkham Ride EWKG RG40 .... 69 F2
Barkham Rd WHIT RG2 .... 62 B5
WWKG RG41 .... 68 D1
Barkham St EWKG RG40 .... 69 F1
Barkhart Dr EWKG RG40 .... 64 D1
Barkhart Gdns EWKG RG40 .... 64 D1
Barkwith Cl EARL RG6 .... 52 B3
Barnard Cl CAV/SC RG4 .... 34 B1
Barn Cl RDGW RG30 .... 49 E1
Barn La HEN RG9 .... 5 H2
Barn Owl Wy THLE RG7 .... 57 E5
Barnsdale Rd WHIT RG2 .... 50 C2

Barnwood Cl RDGW RG30 .... 41 F2
Baron Ct RDGW RG30 .... 41 F3
Baronsmead HEN RG9 .... 6 A4
Barracks La THLE RG7 .... 66 A2
Barrett Crs EWKG RG40 .... 65 E2
Barrett's La WHIT RG2 .... 62 A2
Barrington Cl EARL RG6 .... 43 G4
Barrington Wy READ RG1 .... 41 F5
Barry Pl READ RG1 .... 2 D2
Barton Rd CALC RG31 .... 39 E4
Basil Cl EARL RG6 .... 51 E4
Basingstoke Rd THLE RG7 .... 59 H3
WHIT RG2 .... 50 A5
Baskerville La HEN RG9 .... 26 D1
Baskerville Rd CAV/SC RG4 .... 13 F4
Baslow Rd WWKG RG41 .... 53 E3
Basmore La HEN RG9 .... 17 E5
Bassett Cl EARL RG6 .... 51 H5
Bath Rd CALC RG31 .... 47 F1
CAV/SC RG4 .... 36 C4
READ RG1 .... 41 F4
THLE RG7 .... 46 A3
Bathurst Rd WWKG RG41 .... 53 E3
Battle Cl GOR/PANG RG8 .... 9 E2
Battle St READ RG1 .... 2 B4
Batty's Barn Cl EWKG RG40 .... 65 E3
Bay Cl EARL RG6 .... 51 E4
Baydon Dr READ RG1 .... 41 F5
Bayford Dr CALC RG31 .... 48 A1
Bayley Ct WWKG RG41 .... 53 E4
Bayliss Rd WAR/TWY RG10 .... 27 G3
Bay Tree Ri CALC RG31 .... 39 F5
Beaconsfield Wy EARL RG6 .... 51 F3
Beal's La CALC RG31 .... 38 D3
Bean Oak Rd EWKG RG40 .... 65 F2
Bearwood Pth WWKG RG41 .... 52 D3
Bearwood Rd WWKG RG41 .... 53 E5
Beatty Dr RDGW RG30 .... 39 H2
Beauchief Cl EARL RG6 .... 51 E5
Beaufield Cl WODY RG5 .... 44 A3
Beaver Cl WWKG RG41 .... 64 C5
Beaver Wy WODY RG5 .... 45 E3
Beck Ct READ RG1 .... 42 B5
Beckett Cl EWKG RG40 .... 65 F2
Beckford Cl WWKG RG41 .... 54 A4
Beckley Cl GOR/PANG RG8 .... 10 C1
Bec Tithe GOR/PANG RG8 .... 20 B1
Bedford Gdns WWKG RG41 .... 54 A5
Bedford Rd READ RG1 .... 2 A4
Bedfordshire Wy WWKG RG41 .... 63 H2
Beecham Rd RDGW RG30 .... 40 D3
Beech Cl RDGW RG30 .... 57 E4
The Beeches CALC RG31 .... 31 G4
GOR/PANG RG8 .... 8 A4
Beech La EARL RG6 .... 51 F2
GOR/PANG RG8 .... 10 B1
Beechnut Cl WWKG RG41 .... 64 A3
Beech Ri CAV/SC RG4 .... 13 F3
Beech Rd CAV/SC RG4 .... 23 E5
GOR/PANG RG8 .... 30 D2
WHIT RG2 .... 50 B3
Beechwood Av CALC RG31 .... 39 G2
WODY RG5 .... 44 A3
Beechwood Cl GOR/PANG RG8 .... 10 A3
Beeson Cl GOR/PANG RG8 .... 10 C1
Beeston Wy EARL RG6 .... 51 F5
Beggars Hill Rd WODY RG5 .... 45 E1
Beighton Cl EARL RG6 .... 51 E5
Bell Ct WAR/TWY RG10 .... 37 G2
Belle Av EARL RG6 .... 43 F5
Belle Vue Rd HEN RG9 .... 16 A1
READ RG1 .... 2 B6
Bell Foundry La EWKG RG40 .... 54 D5
Bell House Gdns EWKG RG40 .... 64 C2
Bellisle GOR/PANG RG8 .... 31 E2

Bell La *HEN* RG9 ...... 6 B3
Bell St *HEN* RG9 ...... 6 B4
Belmont Rd *RDGW* RG30.... 41 E3
Belvedere Wk *WWKG* RG41 .... 52 D2
Bembridge Pl *READ* RG1 .... 3 H5 🔲
Bennet Rd *WHIT* RG2.... 49 H4
Bennett's Hl *WHIT* RG2 .... 57 E1
Benning Wy *EWKG* RG40 .... 54 D5
Bensgrove Cl *GOR/PANG* RG8 .... 10 C1 🔲
Benson Rd *WHIT* RG2 .... 50 C2
Benyon Ct *READ* RG1.... 41 F4
Bere Court Rd *GOR/PANG* RG8.... 29 E5
Beresford Rd *RDGW* RG30 .... 41 F2
Berkeley Av *READ* RG1 .... 41 F4
Berkshire Circular Routes
GOR/PANG RG8 ...... 30 A5
Berkshire Dr *CALC* RG31 .... 39 F2
Berkshire Rd *HEN* RG9 .... 16 A1
Berrylands Rd *CAV/SC* RG4.... 34 A4
Berry's La *RDGW* RG30 .... 48 A4
RDGW RG30 .... 48 C5
Berstead Cl *EARL* RG6 .... 51 G4 🔲
Betam Rd *READ* RG1 .... 3 K5
Betchworth Av *EARL* RG6.... 51 F2
Betty Grove La *WWKG* RG41.... 62 C1
Beverley Gdns *WAR/TWY* RG10 .... 27 H3
Beverley Rd *CALC* RG31 .... 39 F1
Bexley Ct *RDGW* RG30 .... 41 E4
Bibury Cl *WODY* RG5 .... 52 A1
Bideford Cl *WODY* RG5 .... 43 H5
Bigbury Gdns *WHIT* RG2 .... 50 B2
Biggs La *EWKG* RG40 .... 68 C3
Billing Av *EWKG* RG40 .... 69 H5
Binbrook Cl *EARL* RG6 .... 52 A3
Binfield Rd *EWKG* RG40 .... 65 C1
Bingley Gv *WODY* RG5 .... 44 C1
Birch Av *RDGW* RG30 .... 40 B2
Birch Cl *CAV/SC* RG4.... 13 G5
Birchen Cl *GOR/PANG* RG8 .... 10 C1 🔲
Birchmead *WWKG* RG30 .... 53 G3
Birch Rd *EWKG* RG40 .... 70 B4
THLE RG7 .... 56 C5
Birch Side *CWTH* RG45 .... 71 G5
Birch Vw *WHIT* RG2 .... 50 C3
Birchwood Cl *CAV/SC* RG4.... 34 B1 🔲
The Birchwoods *CALC* RG31 .... 39 E2
Birdhill Av *WHIT* RG2 .... 50 C3
Bird Ms *EWKG* RG40 .... 64 C2 🔲
Bird Wood Ct *CAV/SC* RG4 .... 13 H5
Birkhall Cl *CALC* RG31 .... 39 F5 🔲
Biscuit Wy *WHIT* RG2.... 49 G5
Bishops Dr *EWKG* RG40 .... 64 D1
Bishop's Rd *EARL* RG6 .... 43 F4
Bitterne Av *CALC* RG31 .... 39 E4
Blackbird Cl *THLE* RG7 .... 57 E5 🔲
Blackley Cl *EARL* RG6 .... 52 B2 🔲
Blackmore La *CAV/SC* RG4 .... 13 H4
Blackthorn Cl *CALC* RG31 .... 31 G5
EARL RG6 .... 43 F3
Blackwater Cl *CAV/SC* RG4 .... 34 D3
THLE RG7 .... 66 A2
Blackwater Ri *CALC* RG31 .... 46 D1 🔲
Blaenavon *CAV/SC* RG4.... 33 G2
Blagdon Rd *WHIT* RG2 .... 50 C3
Blagrave Farm La *CAV/SC* RG4.... 33 F3
Blagrave La *CAV/SC* RG4 .... 32 D4
Blagrave Ri *CALC* RG31 .... 39 F4
Blagrave St *READ* RG1 .... 3 F4
Blagrove La *WWKG* RG41 .... 64 A4
Blake Cl *EWKG* RG40 .... 55 F5
Blakes Cottages *READ* RG1 .... 3 H5
Blakes Rd *WAR/TWY* RG10 .... 27 H1
Blanchard Cl *WODY* RG5 .... 45 E2
Blandford Dr *WWKG* RG41 .... 63 H1
Blandford Rd *WHIT* RG2 .... 50 B5
Blandy Rd *HEN* RG9 .... 16 A1
Blandy's La *GOR/PANG* RG8 .... 28 A1
Blatch's Cl *THLE* RG7 .... 46 A2 🔲
Blenheim Cl *WWKG* RG41 .... 63 H2 🔲
Blenheim Gdns *READ* RG1 .... 42 D4
Blenheim Rd *CAV/SC* RG4 .... 33 H3
READ RG1 .... 42 C3
Blewbury Dr *CALC* RG31 .... 39 E3
Blossom Av *THLE* RG7 .... 46 B2
Blossom La *THLE* RG7 .... 46 B2
Blounts Court Rd *CAV/SC* RG4 .... 13 H5
Bluebell Dr *THLE* RG7 .... 56 C5
Bluebell Meadow *WWKG* RG41 .... 53 F2
Blundells Rd *RDGW* RG30 .... 39 H2
Bobgreen Ct *WHIT* RG2 .... 60 B2 🔲
Bodmin Rd *WODY* RG5 .... 43 H5
Body Rd *READ* RG1 .... 2 D6
Bolney La *HEN* RG9 .... 16 D4
Bolney Rd *HEN* RG9 .... 17 E5
Bolney Trevor Dr *HEN* RG9.... 16 D5
Bones La *HEN* RG9 .... 25 F1
Boot End *WHIT* RG2 .... 49 G5
Booth Dr *EWKG* RG40 .... 69 H2

Borrowdale Rd *WWKG* RG41 .... 53 E1
Bosham Cl *EARL* RG6 .... 51 G5 🔲
Boston Av *READ* RG1.... 41 G5
Boston Rd *HEN* RG9.... 16 B1
Bosworth Gdns *WODY* RG5 .... 52 B1
The Bothy *WAR/TWY* RG10 .... 27 G2
Bottisham Cl *EARL* RG6 .... 51 H5 🔲
Bottom La *THLE* RG7 .... 46 B5
Boulton Rd *WHIT* RG2 .... 50 A2
Boult St *READ* RG1 .... 3 H6
Boundary Cl *CALC* RG31 .... 39 F4 🔲
Boundary La *CAV/SC* RG4 .... 33 F4
Bourne Av *WHIT* RG2 .... 50 A1
Bourne Cl *CALC* RG31 .... 47 F1
Bourne Rd *GOR/PANG* RG8 .... 30 B2
Bourne-Stevens Cl *READ* RG1 .... 3 G6
Bourton Cl *RDGW* RG30.... 40 A3
Bowfell Cl *CALC* RG31 .... 31 F5 🔲
Bowling Ct *HEN* RG9 .... 5 H3
Bowling Green La
GOR/PANG RG8 .... 31 E2
Bowyer Crs *EWKG* RG40 .... 54 D5
Bracken Cl *CALC* RG31 .... 39 F1 🔲
Brackendale Wy *EARL* RG6.... 43 F5
The Brackens *CWTH* RG45 .... 71 H4
Brackstone Cl *CAV/SC* RG4 .... 34 B5
Brading Wy *GOR/PANG* RG8 .... 31 G2
Bradley Dr *EWKG* RG40 .... 70 B2
Bradmore Wy *EARL* RG6 .... 51 F5
Bradwell Rd *CALC* RG31 .... 31 F5 🔲
Bramber Ms *CAV/SC* RG4 .... 34 D3 🔲
Bramble Crs *RDGW* RG30 .... 39 H3
Bramblegate *CWTH* RG45 .... 71 H5
The Brambles *CWTH* RG45 .... 71 E5
Bramblings *CAV/SC* RG4 .... 33 F1
Bramley Cl *EARL* RG6 .... 51 F2
Bramley Crs *CAV/SC* RG4 .... 13 F4 🔲
Brampton Cha *HEN* RG9 .... 16 D5
Bramshaw Rd *RDGW* RG30 .... 40 B1
Bramshill Cl *WHIT* RG2 .... 68 B3
Bran Cl *RDGW* RG30 .... 39 H2
Brandon Av *WODY* RG5 .... 44 D1
Brants Cl *WHIT* RG2 .... 68 B1 🔲
Braybrooke Gdns
WAR/TWY RG10 .... 27 G3
Braybrooke Rd *WAR/TWY* RG10 .... 27 G3
Brayford Rd *WHIT* RG2 .... 50 B5
Bray Rd *RDGW* RG30 .... 48 C1
Brean Wk *EARL* RG6 .... 51 F3
Brecon Rd *WODY* RG5 .... 44 C2
Bredon Rd *WWKG* RG41 .... 54 A4
Breedons Hl *GOR/PANG* RG8 .... 29 H2
Brendon Cl *RDGW* RG30 .... 39 H1 🔲
Brent Gdns *WHIT* RG2 .... 50 A2
Brerewood *EARL* RG6 .... 51 E3
Briant's Av *CAV/SC* RG4.... 34 B5
Briar Cl *CAV/SC* RG4 .... 33 H3
Briars Cl *GOR/PANG* RG8 .... 30 B2
Briarwood Dr *EWKG* RG40 .... 69 H5 🔲
Bridges Cl *WWKG* RG41 .... 64 A1
Bridge St *READ* RG1 .... 2 E6
READ RG1 .... 33 H5
Bridgewater Cl *RDGW* RG30 .... 40 D1 🔲
Bridle Pth *GOR/PANG* RG8 .... 10 B1 🔲
Bridle Rd *GOR/PANG* RG8 .... 20 B1 🔲
Bridport Cl *EARL* RG6 .... 52 A3
Brierley Pl *CALC* RG31 .... 31 F3 🔲
Brigham Rd *READ* RG1 .... 2 E2
Brighton Rd *EARL* RG6 .... 43 F4
Brill Cl *CAV/SC* RG4 .... 33 H3
Brimblecombe Cl *WWKG* RG41 .... 54 B4
Brimpton Rd *RDGW* RG30 .... 48 C1
Brinds Cl *CAV/SC* RG4 .... 13 G4
Brisbane Rd *RDGW* RG30 .... 40 C5
Britten Rd *READ* RG1 .... 50 A1
Brixham Rd *WHIT* RG2 .... 50 A3
Broad Hinton *WAR/TWY* RG10 .... 37 H5
Broadlands Cl *CALC* RG31 .... 39 G5
Broadmoor La *CAV/SC* RG4 .... 33 E3
Broad St *EWKG* RG40 .... 64 D2
READ RG1 .... 2 E4
Broadwater La *WAR/TWY* RG10.... 45 H1
Broadwater Rd *WAR/TWY* RG10 .... 37 H4
Brock Gdns *RDGW* RG30 .... 40 D2
Brockley Cl *RDGW* RG30 .... 40 B2
Brocks Wy *HEN* RG9 .... 26 D1
Brompton Cl *EARL* RG6 .... 52 A4 🔲
Brook Cl *WWKG* RG41 .... 54 B5
Brooker's Hl *WHIT* RG2 .... 60 C2
Brooklyn Dr *CAV/SC* RG4 .... 24 A5
The Brookmill *READ* RG1 .... 49 F1
Brooksby Rd *CALC* RG31 .... 31 G5
Brookside *WWKG* RG41 .... 64 A1
Brookside Cl *EARL* RG6 .... 52 A2
Brook St *WAR/TWY* RG10 .... 37 G3
Brook St West *READ* RG1 .... 2 D7
Broom Cl *CALC* RG31 .... 39 F5 🔲

Broomfield Rd *RDGW* RG30 .... 40 A2
Broom Gv *WWKG* RG41 .... 63 G4
Broughton Cl *RDGW* RG30 .... 40 D1 🔲
Brownlow Rd *READ* RG1.... 2 A6
Bruce Rd *WODY* RG5 .... 44 A3
Brunel Dr *WODY* RG5 .... 44 C1
Brunel Rd *THLE* RG7 .... 46 B3
RDGW RG30 .... 48 B1
Brunswick St *READ* RG1 .... 2 A7
Bryant Pl *GOR/PANG* RG8 .... 31 E2 🔲
Brybur Cl *WHIT* RG2 .... 50 C5
Buccaneer Cl *WODY* RG5 .... 45 E2 🔲
Buchanan Dr *EWKG* RG40 .... 69 H4
Buckden Cl *WODY* RG5 .... 44 D4
Buckhurst Gv *EWKG* RG40 .... 65 G3
Buckhurst Wy *EARL* RG6 .... 51 F2
Buckingham Dr *CAV/SC* RG4 .... 34 A2
Buckland Rd *WHIT* RG2 .... 50 A2
Bucknell Av *GOR/PANG* RG8 .... 30 B2
Bucknell Cl *CALC* RG31 .... 48 A1
Buck Side *READ* RG1 .... 33 H5
Buckthorn Cl *EWKG* RG40 .... 65 F1 🔲
Budge's Gdns *EWKG* RG40 .... 65 E1
Budge's Rd *EWKG* RG40 .... 65 E1
Bulmershe Ct *EARL* RG6 .... 43 G4
Bulmershe Rd *READ* RG1 .... 42 D4
Bunce's La *GOR/PANG* RG8 .... 20 D2
Bungler's Hl *THLE* RG7 .... 67 G5
Burbidge Cl *CALC* RG31 .... 48 A2 🔲
Burchett Coppice *EWKG* RG40 .. 70 A3 🔲
Burcombe Wy *CAV/SC* RG4.... 34 A3
Burford Ct *EWKG* RG40 .... 65 F3
Burgess Cl *WODY* RG5 .... 44 A5
Burghfield Rd *RDGW* RG30 .... 48 B1 🔲
Burleigh Ms *CAV/SC* RG4 .... 34 B1 🔲
Burlingham Cl *WHIT* RG2 .... 60 B2 🔲
Burlington Rd *RDGW* RG30.... 39 G3
Burnham Ri *CAV/SC* RG4 .... 24 B5
Burniston Cl *EARL* RG6 .... 52 B3 🔲
Burns Cl *WODY* RG5 .... 52 B1
Burnthouse Br *RDGW* RG30 .... 58 B3
Burnthouse La *RDGW* RG30 .... 58 C1
Burnt Oak *EWKG* RG40 .... 70 A3 🔲
Burrcroft Rd *RDGW* RG30 .... 40 B5
Burton Cl *WAR/TWY* RG10 .... 37 H5
Burwell Cl *EARL* RG6 .... 51 H4
Bute St *RDGW* RG30 .... 40 C5
Butlers Orch *CAV/SC* RG4 .... 23 E1
Butlers Pond *GOR/PANG* RG8 .... 20 A2
Buttenshaw Av *WHIT* RG2 .... 68 C3
Buttenshaw Cl *WHIT* RG2 .... 68 D3
Buttercup Cl *EWKG* RG40 .... 65 G2
Butter Market *READ* RG1 .... 3 F5
Butts Hill Rd *WODY* RG5 .... 44 B1
Buxton Av *CAV/SC* RG4 .... 33 G3
Byefield Rd *RDGW* RG30 .... 48 B1
Byreton Cl *EARL* RG6 .... 51 G3
Byron Rd *EARL* RG6 .... 43 F3
WAR/TWY RG10 .... 37 H3
Bythorn Cl *EARL* RG6 .... 52 B3
Byworth Cl *WHIT* RG2 .... 50 A5

C

Cadogan Cl *CAV/SC* RG4 .... 34 D3 🔲
RDGW RG30 .... 39 H3 🔲
Caistor Cl *CALC* RG31 .... 47 E1 🔲
Calbourne Dr *CALC* RG31 .... 47 G1 🔲
Calcot Place Dr *CALC* RG31 .... 47 H1
Caldbeck Dr *WODY* RG5 .... 44 C4
Calder Cl *RDGW* RG30 .... 40 A3
Caleta Cl *CAV/SC* RG4 .... 34 C5 🔲
Callington Rd *WHIT* RG2 .... 50 A4
Calshot Pl *CALC* RG31 .... 47 G1 🔲
Cambrian Wy *CALC* RG31 .... 47 G1
EWKG RG40 .... 70 B3
Cambridgeshire Cl
WWKG RG41 .... 63 H2 🔲
Cambridge St *READ* RG1.... 2 A4
Camden Pl *CALC* RG31 .... 47 E1 🔲
Camelford Cl *WHIT* RG2 .... 50 A4
Camellia Wy *WWKG* RG41 .... 63 G1 🔲
Campbell Rd *WODY* RG5 .... 44 A5
Campion Wy *EWKG* RG40 .... 65 F1
Canal Wy *READ* RG1 .... 3 K5
Cannock Wy *EARL* RG6 .... 51 H4
Cannon St *READ* RG1 .... 2 A4
Canterbury Rd *WHIT* RG2 .... 50 A2
Cantley Crs *WWKG* RG41 .... 54 B5
Caraway Rd *EARL* RG6.... 51 F5
Cardiff Rd *READ* RG1 .... 2 A2
Cardigan Rd *READ* RG1 .... 42 D4
Cardinal Cl *READ* RG1 .... 34 A5 🔲
Carew Cl *CALC* RG31 .... 31 E3 🔲
Carey Rd *EWKG* RG40.... 64 D3
Carey St *READ* RG1 .... 2 C6

Carisbrooke Cl *CAV/SC* RG4 .... 34 B1 🔲
Carland Cl *EARL* RG6 51
Carlile Gdns *WAR/TWY* RG10 27
Carling Rd *CAV/SC* RG4 13
Carlisle Rd *CALC* RG31 31
Carlton Cl *WODY* RG5.... 44
Carlton Rd *CAV/SC* RG4 33
Carnarvon Rd *READ* RG1 42
Carolina Pl *EWKG* RG40 69
Caroline Dr *WWKG* RG41 64
Caroline St *READ* RG1 2
Carrick Gdns *WODY* RG5 43
Carron Cl *RDGW* RG30 40
Carsdale Cl *READ* RG1 41
Carshalton Wy *EARL* RG6 51
Carston Gv *CALC* RG31 48
Carter's Hl *EWKG* RG40 55
Carters Ri *CALC* RG31 47
Cartmel Dr *WODY* RG5.... 44
Cassia Dr *EARL* RG6 .... 51 E4 🔲
Castle Crs *READ* RG1 2
Castle Hl *READ* RG1 2
THLE RG7 67
Castle St *READ* RG1 2
Catalina Cl *WODY* RG5 45
Catcliffe Wy *EARL* RG6 51
Catherine St *RDGW* RG30 41
The Causeway *CAV/SC* RG4 3
Causmans Wy *CALC* RG31 39
Cavalier Cl *THLE* RG7 46
Cavendish Gdns *WWKG* RG41.... 52
Cavendish Rd *CAV/SC* RG4 34
Caversham Br *READ* RG1 33
Caversham Park Dr *CAV/SC* RG4.. 34
Caversham Park Rd *CAV/SC* RG4.. 34
Caversham Rd *READ* RG1 2
Cawsam Gdns *CAV/SC* RG4 34
Caxton Cl *RDGW* RG30.... 40
Cecil Aldin Dr *CALC* RG31 31
Cedar Cl *EWKG* RG40 64
Cedar Dr *GOR/PANG* RG8 29
Cedar Rd *WHIT* RG2 50
The Cedars *CALC* RG31 31
Cedar Wood Crs *CAV/SC* RG4 34
Central Wk *EWKG* RG40 .... 64 D2
Century Dr *THLE* RG7 66
Chaffinch Cl *CALC* RG31 .... 39 E3
WWKG RG41 63
Chagford Rd *WHIT* RG2.... 50
Chain St *READ* RG1 2
Chalcraft Cl *HEN* RG9.... 15
Chalfont Cl *EARL* RG6 51
Chalfont Wy *EARL* RG6 .... 51 F5
Chalgrove Wy *CAV/SC* RG4 34
Chalk Hl *HEN* RG9 15
Chalkhouse Green La
CAV/SC RG4 23
Chalkhousegreen La
CAV/SC RG4 24
Chalkhouse Green Rd
CAV/SC RG4 23
Challenor Cl *EWKG* RG40 .... 70 A4
Chamberlain's Gdns *WHIT* RG2 .. 68 B1
Champion Rd *CAV/SC* RG4 3
The Chancellor's Wy *EARL* RG6 50
Chapel Hl *CALC* RG31 39
Chapel La *THLE* RG7 66
Chard Cl *WODY* RG5 44
Charles Evans Wy *CAV/SC* RG4 34
Charles St *READ* RG1 2
Charlton Cl *EWKG* RG40 .... 70 A3
Charlville Dr *CALC* RG31 .... 47 E1
Charndon Cl *WHIT* RG2 42
Charrington Rd *CALC* RG31 47
Charvil House Rd
WAR/TWY RG10 36
Charvil La *CAV/SC* RG4.... 36
Charvil Meadow Rd
WAR/TWY RG10 37
Charwood Rd *EWKG* RG40 65
Chaseside Av *WAR/TWY* RG10 37
The Chase *CALC* RG31 47
CWTH RG45 71
Chatham St *READ* RG1 2
Chatsworth Av *WWKG* RG41 52
Chatsworth Cl *CAV/SC* RG4 34
Chatteris Wy *EARL* RG6 51
The Chatters *THLE* RG7 67
Chatton Cl *EARL* RG6 51
Chaucer Cl *CAV/SC* RG4 33
EWKG RG40 .... 65 G2
Chaucer Wy *WWKG* RG41 .... 63 H3
Chazey Cl *CAV/SC* RG4 22
Chazey Rd *CAV/SC* RG4 33
Cheapside *READ* RG1.... 2
Cheddington Cl *RDGW* RG30 .... 40 A4
Cheeseman Cl *EWKG* RG40 .... 65 E1
Chelsea Cl *RDGW* RG30 40

elwood Rd *EARL* RG6 .... 51 G3
epstow Rd *CALC* RG31 .... 31 F5
equers Wy *WODY* RG5 .... 43 H3
eriton Av *WAR/TWY* RG10 ...... 37 C5
eriton Pl *CAV/SC* RG4 .... 13 C4 ⬚
erry Cl *CAV/SC* RG4 .... 24 B4
erry Tree Gv *WWKG* RG41 ...... 63 G4 ⬚
esterman St *READ* RG1 .... 42 A4 ⬚
esterment Wy *EARL* RG6 .... 52 A4
ester St *CAV/SC* RG4 .... 33 H5
RDGW RG30 .... 34 D2
estnut Av *CAV/SC* RG4 .... 34 D3 ⬚
WWKG RG41 .... 63 H1
estnut Cl *THLE* RG7 .... 46 B1 ⬚
estnut Crs *WHIT* RG2 .... 60 D4
estnut Dr *RDGW* RG30 .... 57 F4
estnut Gv *GOR/PANG* RG8 ...... 31 G2
e Chestnuts *HEN* RG9 .... 26 D1
etwode Cl *EWKG* RG40 .... 65 F2 ⬚
eviot Dr *WAR/TWY* RG10 .... 37 E3
ichester Rd *RDGW* RG30 .... 39 H2
icory Cl *EARL* RG6 .... 51 E4
ieveley Cl *CALC* RG31 .... 39 F2
ilcombe Wy *EARL* RG6 .... 52 A3
ild Cl *EWKG* RG40 .... 55 E5
ildrey Wy *CALC* RG31 .... 39 E2
iltern Cl *HEN* RG9 .... 15 G1
iltern Ct *CAV/SC* RG4 .... 34 A1
iltern Crs *EARL* RG6 .... 43 F3
iltern Dr *WAR/TWY* RG10 .... 37 E3
iltern Rd *CAV/SC* RG4 .... 34 B3
HEN RG9 .... 13 F2
iltern Vw *GOR/PANG* RG8 ...... 31 G2
ippenham Cl *EARL* RG6 .... 51 E5 ⬚
ittering Cl *EARL* RG6 .... 51 H4
ittern Rd *EARL* RG6 .... 51 H4
ivers Dr *EWKG* RG40 .... 69 H4 ⬚
olmeley Pl *READ* RG1 .... 42 D3 ⬚
olmeley Rd *READ* RG1 .... 42 D2
olmeley Ter *READ* RG1 .... 42 D3 ⬚
ristchurch Gdns *WHIT* RG2 .... 42 B5
ristchurch Rd *WHIT* RG2 ...... 42 B5
udleigh Gdns *WHIT* RG2 ...... 50 B3
urch Cl *HEN* RG9 .... 4 C5
WWKG RG41 .... 53 F3 ⬚
urch End La *RDGW* RG30 ...... 40 A3
urch Hams *EWKG* RG40 .... 69 G5
urch Hl *WAR/TWY* RG10 .... 45 H3
urchill Crs *CAV/SC* RG4 .... 13 G3
urchill Dr *WWKG* RG41 .... 53 E3
urch La *EWKG* RG40 .... 69 F2
HEN RG9 .... 13 G1
HEN RG9 .... 26 C3
READ RG1 .... 3 F7
THLE RG7 .... 68 A5
RDGW RG30 .... 57 H2
WHIT RG2 .... 60 C3
WHIT RG2 .... 61 H4
urch Ms *GOR/PANG* RG8 .... 31 G2 ⬚
WODY RG5 .... 44 C2
urch Rd *EARL* RG6 .... 43 C5
WODY RG5 .... 44 C2
urch St *CAV/SC* RG4 .... 33 H5
HEN RG9 .... 6 A5
READ RG1 .... 3 F7
THLE RG7 .... 46 A2
WAR/TWY RG10 .... 27 F2
WAR/TWY RG10 .... 37 G3
nnamon Cl *EARL* RG6 .... 51 E4 ⬚
ntra Av *WHIT* RG2 .... 50 A1
rcuit La *RDGW* RG30 .... 40 D5
ty Rd *CALC* RG31 .... 39 F3
anfield Crs *CALC* RG31 .... 31 F5
are Av *EWKG* RG40 .... 64 D1
are Ct *EWKG* RG40 .... 64 D1
arence Rd *HEN* RG9 .... 6 A4
arence Wy *CALC* RG31 .... 47 E1
arendon Cl *WWKG* RG41 .... 53 C3
arendon Rd *EARL* RG6 .... 43 F4
ares Green Rd *THLE* RG7 ...... 60 C5
RDGW RG30 .... 48 C1 ⬚
ayhill Rd *THLE* RG7 .... 56 C5
ay La *EWKG* RG40 .... 65 G2
ent Rd *WHIT* RG2 .... 50 A1
evedon Dr *EARL* RG6 .... 51 F3
evedon Rd *CALC* RG31 .... 31 H4
eveland *WAR/TWY* RG10 .... 37 E3 ⬚
evemede *GOR/PANG* RG8 .... 8 B2 ⬚
ifton Park Rd *CAV/SC* RG4 .... 33 G4
ifton Ri *WAR/TWY* RG10 .... 27 H3
ifton Rd *WWKG* RG41 .... 54 B5
ifton St *READ* RG1 .... 2 B6
ivedale Rd *WODY* RG5 .... 52 A3

Cloister Ms *THLE* RG7 .... 46 B2 ⬚
The Cloisters *CAV/SC* RG4 ...... 33 H4
The Close *GOR/PANG* RG8 ...... 10 C1 ⬚
  HEN RG9 .... 16 A1
  THLE RG7 .... 56 D5
  WODY RG5 .... 44 B5
Clove Cl *EARL* RG6 .... 51 F5
Clover Cl *WODY* RG40 .... 65 F1
Coalport Wy *RDGW* RG30 .... 39 H1
Cobham Rd *WODY* RG5 .... 44 C3
Cockney Hl *RDGW* RG30 .... 40 A4
Cody Cl *WODY* RG5 .... 45 E2
Coldharbour Cl *HEN* RG9 .... 15 H1
Coldicutt St *CAV/SC* RG4 .... 3 H1
Colemans Moor La *WODY* RG5 .. 44 C4
Colemans Moor Rd *WODY* RG5 44 C5
Coleridge La *GOR/PANG* RG8 .. 28 C3
Coley Av *READ* RG1 .... 41 C4
Coley Hl *READ* RG1 .... 2 C7
Coley Park Rd *READ* RG1 .... 2 C7
Coley Pl *READ* RG1 .... 2 D7
College Rd *EARL* RG6 .... 43 E4
Colleton Dr *WAR/TWY* RG10 ... 37 H4
Colliers La *HEN* RG9 .... 13 F1
Colliers Wy *RDGW* RG30 .... 40 C3
Collis St *READ* RG1 .... 42 A5
Colmore La *HEN* RG9 .... 13 F1
Colmworth Cl *EARL* RG6 .... 51 F5 ⬚
Colston Cl *CALC* RG31 .... 47 C1 ⬚
Coltsfoot Cl *THLE* RG7 .... 57 E5
Columbia Ct *EWKG* RG40 ...... 69 H4 ⬚
Colyton Wy *GOR/PANG* RG8 ... 31 F2
Combe Rd *RDGW* RG30 .... 40 A3
Comet Wy *WODY* RG5 .... 44 D3
Comfrey Cl *EWKG* RG40 .... 55 F5
Commercial Rd *WHIT* RG2 ...... 42 A4
Commonfield La *EWKG* RG40 .. 69 E3
Commons Rd *WWKG* RG41 ...... 54 A4
Compton Av *EARL* RG6 .... 39 E3
Compton Cl *EARL* RG6 .... 51 H1
Concorde Wy *WODY* RG5 .... 44 D3 ⬚
Condor Cl *CALC* RG31 .... 31 F4
Conifer Dr *CALC* RG31 .... 31 E5
The Conifers *CWTH* RG45 ...... 71 H4
Coningham Rd *WHIT* RG2 ...... 60 B2
Conisboro Av *CAV/SC* RG4 ..... 33 F2
Conisboro Wy *CAV/SC* RG4 .... 33 F2
Coniston Cl *WODY* RG5 .... 44 B5
Coniston Dr *RDGW* RG30 .... 32 A5
Connaught Cl *RDGW* RG30 .... 41 E3 ⬚
Connaught Rd *RDGW* RG30 .... 41 E3
Constable Cl *WODY* RG5 .... 45 E2 ⬚
Constitution Rd *RDGW* RG30 .. 40 C2 ⬚
Consul Cl *WODY* RG5 .... 44 D5
Conway Rd *CALC* RG31 .... 39 F5
Conygree Cl *EARL* RG6 .... 51 G4
Coombes La *WWKG* RG41 .... 63 F4
Cooper Cl *WHIT* RG2 .... 60 B1
Cooper Rd *HEN* RG9 .... 5 H3
Coopers Pightle *CAV/SC* RG4 .. 23 E1
Copenhagen Cl *WHIT* RG2 ..... 60 B1 ⬚
Copperdale Cl *WHIT* RG2 .... 50 D2
Coppice Rd *WODY* RG5 .... 52 B1
Copse Av *CAV/SC* RG4 .... 34 A4
Copse Cl *CALC* RG31 .... 31 C4
Copse Dr *WWKG* RG41 .... 64 B1
Copse Md *WODY* RG5 .... 44 C1
The Copse *WAR/TWY* RG10 ..... 27 H4
Copse Wy *EWKG* RG40 .... 69 H4 ⬚
Corbett Gdns *WODY* RG5 .... 44 B3
Corbridge Rd *WHIT* RG2 .... 50 B2
Corby Cl *WODY* RG5 .... 44 D1
Corfe Ms *CAV/SC* RG4 .... 34 A4
Corfield Gn *WWKG* RG41 .... 54 A5 ⬚
Coriander Wy *EARL* RG6 .... 51 E4 ⬚
Corinne Cl *WHIT* RG2 .... 50 A4
Cornfield Wy *WODY* RG5 .... 44 D2
Cornflower Cl *WWKG* RG41 .... 63 G1 ⬚
Cornwall Cl *WWKG* RG41 ...... 63 G2 ⬚
Cornwood Gdns *WHIT* RG2 ..... 50 A4
Coronation Sq *EWKG* RG40 .... 65 E1 ⬚
  RDGW RG30 .... 48 C1 ⬚
Corsham Rd *CALC* RG31 .... 48 A2 ⬚
Corwen Rd *RDGW* RG30 .... 39 G2
Cotswold Wy *CALC* RG31 .... 31 F5
Cottesmore Rd *WODY* RG5 ..... 44 A4
Courage Ct *RDGW* RG30 .... 40 C5 ⬚
Courtenay Dr *CAV/SC* RG4 ..... 24 A5
Courtlands Hl *GOR/PANG* RG8 29 H3
Courts Rd *EARL* RG6 .... 51 G1
The Courtyard *THLE* RG7 .... 46 B2
Coventry Rd *READ* RG1 .... 42 D3
Cow La *READ* RG1 .... 2 A1
  RDGW RG30 .... 2 A3
Cowper Wy *RDGW* RG30 .... 49 E1 ⬚
Cradock Rd *WHIT* RG2 .... 49 H1
Craig Av *RDGW* RG30 .... 40 C2
Crail Cl *WWKG* RG41 .... 64 B5

Cranbourne Av *CALC* RG31 ..... 47 F1 ⬚
Cranbourne Gdns *RDGW* RG30 . 32 A5
Cranbury Rd *RDGW* RG30 .... 41 E3
Crane Whf *READ* RG1 .... 3 C5
Cranmer Cl *CALC* RG31 .... 31 E4
Craven Av *READ* RG1 .... 3 K6
Crawford Cl *EARL* RG6 .... 51 G2
Crawshay Dr *CAV/SC* RG4 ...... 24 A5
Craysleaze *CAV/SC* RG4 .... 23 E1
Crecy Cl *WWKG* RG41 .... 63 H2 ⬚
Crediton Cl *WODY* RG5 .... 44 D4
Cremyll Rd *READ* RG1 .... 2 B1
Crescent Cl *CALC* RG31 .... 39 G1
  EWKG RG40 .... 64 D3
  READ RG1 .... 42 D4
The Crescent *EARL* RG6 .... 51 H1
  HEN RG9 .... 17 E5
  THLE RG7 .... 46 B1
Cressingham Rd *WHIT* RG2 .... 50 B3
Crest Ct *WAR/TWY* RG10 .... 37 H1
Creswell Cl *WHIT* RG2 .... 60 A2
Crispin Cl *CAV/SC* RG4 .... 33 E2
Crisp Rd *HEN* RG9 .... 5 H3
Crockhamwell Rd *WODY* RG5 . 44 B4
Crocus Wy *WWKG* RG41 .... 63 G1 ⬚
Croft Cl *WHIT* RG2 .... 70 B1
Croft Rd *EWKG* RG40 .... 70 B1
  GOR/PANG RG8 .... 8 B3
  THLE RG7 .... 66 B1
Croft Wy *GOR/PANG* RG8 .... 10 C1
Cromer Cl *CALC* RG31 .... 39 F1 ⬚
Cromwell Cl *HEN* RG9 .... 16 A1 ⬚
Cromwell Rd *CAV/SC* RG4 ...... 34 A5
  HEN RG9 .... 16 B1
Crosfields Cl *WHIT* RG2 .... 50 D5
Crossland Rd *READ* RG1 .... 3 F6
Cross St *EWKG* RG40 .... 64 D2 ⬚
  READ RG1 .... 3 F5
Crown La *THLE* RG7 .... 46 B2 ⬚
Crown Pl *READ* RG1 .... 3 H7
Crown St *READ* RG1 .... 3 F7
Crowsley Rd *HEN* RG9 .... 16 D5
Crowsley Wy *CAV/SC* RG4 ...... 13 F4
Crutchley Rd *EWKG* RG40 ...... 64 D1
Cuddesdon Cl *GOR/PANG* RG8 10 C1 ⬚
Culford Cl *EARL* RG6 .... 52 A3
Culloden Wy *WWKG* RG41 ...... 63 H1
Culver La *EARL* RG6 .... 43 F4
Culver Rd *READ* RG1 .... 43 E4
Cumberland Rd *READ* RG1 ..... 42 C2
Cumberland Wy *WWKG* RG41 . 63 G2 ⬚
Curlew Dr *CALC* RG31 .... 39 F4
Curleys Wy *THLE* RG7 .... 66 C5 ⬚
Curl Wy *WWKG* RG41 .... 64 B3
Curtis Cl *CALC* RG31 .... 39 E5
Curzon St *RDGW* RG30 .... 41 E2
Cutbush Cl *EARL* RG6 .... 51 G5
Cutbush La *EARL* RG6 .... 51 F5
  WHIT RG2 .... 60 D2
Cwmcarn *CAV/SC* RG4 .... 33 C1
Cypress Cl *EWKG* RG40 .... 70 B3
Cypress Rd *WODY* RG5 .... 44 D4

D

Dacre Av *CAV/SC* RG4 .... 34 D3
Dale Rd *WHIT* RG2 .... 42 A5
Dalton Cl *RDGW* RG30 .... 39 H2 ⬚
Damar Gdns *HEN* RG9 .... 16 B1
Danywern Dr *WWKG* RG41 ..... 53 F3
Darby La *GOR/PANG* RG8 .... 28 A2
Darell Rd *CAV/SC* RG4 .... 33 G4
Dark La *CALC* RG31 .... 31 E5
  WAR/TWY RG10 .... 45 H1
Dart Cl *EWKG* RG40 .... 70 A4
Dartington Av *WODY* RG5 ...... 52 A1
Darwin Cl *WHIT* RG2 .... 49 H4
Dauntless Rd *THLE* RG7 .... 57 E5
Davis St *WAR/TWY* RG10 .... 53 G1
Davis Wy *WAR/TWY* RG10 ...... 53 G1
Davy Cl *EWKG* RG40 .... 64 D3
Dawlish Rd *WHIT* RG2 .... 50 B3
Deacon Cl *EWKG* RG40 .... 54 D5
Deacon Wy *RDGW* RG30 .... 39 H1
Deadman's La *GOR/PANG* RG8 . 11 F4
Deanfield Av *HEN* RG9 .... 6 A5
Deanfield Rd *HEN* RG9 .... 5 H5
Dean Gv *EWKG* RG40 .... 3 K1
Deans Farm *CAV/SC* RG4 .... 3 H1
Deansgate Rd *READ* RG1 .... 3 F7
De Beauvoir Rd *READ* RG1 ...... 3 F3
De Bohun Rd *READ* RG1 .... 3 F3
Deepdene Cl *READ* RG1 .... 2 A6
Deerhurst Av *WWKG* RG41 ..... 53 F3
Dee Rd *RDGW* RG30 .... 40 C3
Delafield Dr *CALC* RG31 .... 47 F1

Delamere Rd *EARL* RG6 .... 43 G2
Delane Dr *WWKG* RG41 .... 53 E3
Delaney Cl *RDGW* RG30 .... 40 A2
Delft Cl *RDGW* RG30 .... 40 A2 ⬚
Dell Rd *CALC* RG31 .... 31 F5
The Dell *READ* RG1 .... 3 H1
The Delph *EARL* RG6 .... 52 A3
De Montfort Rd *READ* RG1 .... 2 E2
Denbeigh Pl *READ* RG1 .... 2 C1
Denbury Gdns *WHIT* RG2 .... 50 B5 ⬚
Denby Wy *RDGW* RG30 .... 40 A1
Dene Cl *EARL* RG6 .... 51 F2
Denmark Av *WODY* RG5 .... 44 D1
Denmark Rd *READ* RG1 .... 3 K6
Denmark St *EWKG* RG40 .... 64 C3
Dennose Cl *EARL* RG6 .... 51 F4
Denton Rd *EWKG* RG40 .... 64 D3
Derby Rd *CAV/SC* RG4 .... 34 A4
Derby St *READ* RG1 .... 2 B4
Derrick Cl *CALC* RG31 .... 47 F1 ⬚
Derwent Cl *WWKG* RG41 .... 63 H2 ⬚
Deveron Dr *RDGW* RG30 .... 40 B2
Devil's Hl *HEN* RG9 .... 14 C3
De-vitre Gn *EWKG* RG40 .... 65 G1
Devitt Cl *READ* RG1 .... 63 H2
Devon Cl *WWKG* RG41 .... 63 H2
Devon Dr *CAV/SC* RG4 .... 34 D3
Devonshire Gdns *CALC* RG31 .. 31 E3
Devonshire Pk *WHIT* RG2 ...... 50 D3
Dewe La *RDGW* RG30 .... 48 A5
Diamond Wy *WWKG* RG41 ...... 63 H1 ⬚
Dickens Cl *CAV/SC* RG4 .... 34 C5
Dieppe Cl *WWKG* RG41 .... 63 H2 ⬚
Ditchfield La *EWKG* RG40 ...... 69 H4
The Dittons *EWKG* RG40 .... 70 A5 ⬚
Doddington Cl *EARL* RG6 .... 51 H4
Dodsells Well *EWKG* RG40 ..... 70 A3 ⬚
Dog La *HEN* RG9 .... 13 H1
Doles Hl *WWKG* RG41 .... 63 G5
Doles La *WWKG* RG41 .... 63 H5
Dolphin Cl *WWKG* RG41 .... 53 F4
Donaldson Wy *WODY* RG5 ...... 44 D2
Don Cl *RDGW* RG30 .... 40 B2
Donegal Cl *CAV/SC* RG4 .... 34 A4
Donkin Hl *CAV/SC* RG4 .... 34 B4
Donnington Gdns *READ* RG1 .. 42 C4
Donnington Pl *WWKG* RG41 ... 53 G3 ⬚
Donnington Rd *READ* RG1 ...... 42 C3
Dorchester Ct *RDGW* RG30 .... 40 D3
Dorking Wy *CALC* RG31 .... 46 D1
Dorothy St *READ* RG1 .... 3 F7
Dorset St *RDGW* RG30 .... 40 D2
Dorset Wy *WWKG* RG41 .... 63 H3
Douglas Gra *WAR/TWY* RG10 .. 53 G1
Douglas Rd *CAV/SC* RG4 .... 34 A5
Dove Cl *EARL* RG6 .... 51 E5 ⬚
Dovecote Rd *WHIT* RG2 .... 60 A1
Dovedale Cl *CAV/SC* RG4 .... 33 G4
Dove La *HEN* RG9 .... 13 E1
Dover St *READ* RG1 .... 2 D7
Dowding Cl *WODY* RG5 .... 44 D3 ⬚
Downing Rd *CALC* RG31 .... 39 F2
Downshire Sq *READ* RG1 .... 2 A7
Downs Wy *CALC* RG31 .... 31 F5
Drake Cl *EWKG* RG40 .... 69 H4
Dray's La *HEN* RG9 .... 13 H1
Drayton Rd *RDGW* RG30 .... 40 C2
Dresden Wy *RDGW* RG30 .... 40 A1 ⬚
Drewett Cl *WHIT* RG2 .... 60 B2
Driftway Cl *EARL* RG6 .... 51 H4
The Drive *EARL* RG6 .... 43 F3
Drome Pth *WWKG* RG41 .... 52 D2
Drovers Wy *WODY* RG5 .... 44 B5
Dudley Cl *CALC* RG31 .... 39 H1
Dudley Ms *CALC* RG31 .... 39 H1 ⬚
Duffield Rd *WODY* RG5 .... 44 C1
Duke St *HEN* RG9 .... 6 B4
  READ RG1 .... 3 F5
Dulnan Cl *RDGW* RG30 .... 40 B2
Dulverton Gdns *WHIT* RG2 ..... 50 B3
Dumbarton Wy *CAV/SC* RG4 ... 34 D2
Dunaways Cl *EARL* RG6 .... 52 A2
Dunbar Dr *WODY* RG5 .... 44 D4
Duncan Dr *WWKG* RG41 .... 63 H3
Duncan Gdns *GOR/PANG* RG8 . 31 F3 ⬚
Duncan Rd *WODY* RG5 .... 44 B4
Dundela Cl *WODY* RG5 .... 44 B4
Dunholme Cl *EARL* RG6 .... 52 B3 ⬚
Dunkirk Cl *WWKG* RG41 .... 63 H2 ⬚
Dunluce Gdns *GOR/PANG* RG8 . 30 B2 ⬚
Dunnock Wy *WAR/TWY* RG10 . 27 H1 ⬚
Dunoon Cl *CALC* RG31 .... 47 H1 ⬚
Dunsfold Rd *RDGW* RG30 ...... 40 A3
Dunstall Cl *CALC* RG31 .... 39 G2 ⬚
Dunstans Dr *WWKG* RG41 ..... 53 E3
Dunster Cl *CAV/SC* RG4 .... 34 B1
Dunt Av *WAR/TWY* RG10 .... 53 H1
Dunt La *WAR/TWY* RG10 .... 45 H5

Durand Rd EARL RG6...... 51 F4
Durant Wy CALC RG31...... 31 G4
Durham Cl WHIT RG2...... 50 B5
Dwyer Rd RDGW RG30...... 48 A1
Dyer Rd EWKG RG40...... 65 F1
Dysonswood La CAV/SC RG4... 23 H1

E

Eagle Cl CWTH RG45...... 71 H4
  WWKG RG41...... 64 A3 ▣
Earley Hill Rd EARL RG6...... 43 F5
Earley Pl READ RG1...... 3 F5
Earlsfield Cl CAV/SC RG4... 34 D3
Easby Wy EARL RG6...... 52 A4
Easington Dr EARL RG6...... 52 B3
Eastbury Av CALC RG31...... 39 E2
Eastbury Pk WWKG RG41...... 53 C3
Eastcourt Av EARL RG6...... 43 F4
East Dr CALC RG31...... 39 H5
Eastern Av READ RG1...... 42 D3
Eastfield La GOR/PANG RG8...... 10 B3
  GOR/PANG RG8...... 20 A5
Easthampstead Rd EWKG RG40... 65 E2
Eastheath Av WWKG RG41...... 64 B4
Eastheath Gdns WWKG RG41 ... 64 C5 ▣
East Park Farm Dr
  WAR/TWY RG10...... 37 E3
East St READ RG1...... 3 G6
East View Cl WAR/TWY RG10...... 27 H2
East View Rd WAR/TWY RG10 ...... 27 H2
Eastwood Rd WODY RG5...... 52 B1
Eaton Pl READ RG1...... 2 C5
Ebborn Sq EARL RG6...... 51 H5 ▣
Eccles Cl CAV/SC RG4...... 34 B5 ▣
Edenhall Cl CALC RG31...... 31 G4
Edenham Cl EARL RG6...... 52 B3
Edenham Crs READ RG1...... 41 F5
Eden Wy WWKG RG41...... 53 E4
Edgar Milward Cl RDGW RG30... 40 B1
Edgehill St READ RG1...... 42 A5
Edgewood Cl CWTH RG45...... 71 H4 ▣
Edinburgh Rd RDGW RG30...... 41 E3 ▣
Edward Rd WAR/TWY RG10...... 37 E2
Egerton Rd WHIT RG2...... 50 D4
Egremont Dr EARL RG6...... 51 H2 ▣
  EARL RG6...... 52 A3 ▣
Elan Cl RDGW RG30...... 40 A3
Eldart Cl RDGW RG30...... 40 C3
Elderberry Wy EARL RG6...... 52 A4 ▣
Elder Cl CALC RG31...... 39 F1
Eldon Pl READ RG1...... 3 J6
Eldon Rd READ RG1...... 3 J6
Eldon Sq READ RG1...... 3 J6
Eldon St READ RG1...... 3 K6
Eldon Ter READ RG1...... 3 J6
Elford Cl EARL RG6...... 51 H4 ▣
Elgar Rd WHIT RG2...... 41 H4
Elgar Rd South WHIT RG2...... 50 A1
Elgarth Dr EWKG RG40...... 70 A3 ▣
Eliot Cl CAV/SC RG4...... 33 H3
Elizabeth Cl HEN RG9...... 5 F5
Elizabeth Rd EWKG RG40...... 65 E2
  HEN RG9...... 15 G1
Elizabeth Rout Cl THLE RG7...... 66 B1
Ellerton Cl THLE RG7...... 46 B1 ▣
Ellesmere Cl CAV/SC RG4...... 34 A4
Ellison Wy EWKG RG40...... 64 C2
Ellis's HI WHIT RG2...... 62 C4
Elm Ct CAV/SC RG4...... 13 G5
Elmcroft GOR/PANG RG8...... 8 B4 ▣
Elm Dr RDGW RG30...... 57 E3
Elmhurst Rd GOR/PANG RG8...... 8 B3
  READ RG1...... 42 C5
Elm La EARL RG6...... 51 F4
Elmleigh Ct CAV/SC RG4...... 34 B5 ▣
Elmley Cl WWKG RG41...... 54 A5
Elm Lodge Av RDGW RG30...... 41 E2
Elm Park Rd RDGW RG30...... 41 E3
Elm Rd CAV/SC RG4...... 23 E5
  EARL RG6...... 51 E3
Elms Rd EWKG RG40...... 64 C3
Elmstone Dr CALC RG31...... 39 F1
Elsley Rd CALC RG31...... 31 G4
Elstow Av CAV/SC RG4...... 34 B1
Elstree Cl CALC RG31...... 31 G5
Eltham Av CAV/SC RG4...... 34 D2
Elvaston Wy RDGW RG30...... 40 A3
Elveden Cl EARL RG6...... 52 B3
Elvendon La GOR/PANG RG8...... 9 H2
Elvendon Rd GOR/PANG RG8...... 8 C2
Elyham GOR/PANG RG8...... 31 E2 ▣
Emblen Crs WHIT RG2...... 68 B1
Embrook Wy CALC RG31...... 46 D1 ▣
Emerald Cl WWKG RG41...... 63 H1 ▣
Emma La WAR/TWY RG10...... 27 H2

Emmbrook Rd WWKG RG41...... 54 A5
Emmbrook V WWKG RG41...... 54 B4
Emm Cl WWKG RG41...... 54 A5
Emmer Green Ct CAV/SC RG4... 34 B2
Emmview Cl WWKG RG41...... 64 A1 ▣
Empress Rd CALC RG31...... 39 F5
Enborne Cl READ RG1...... 39 F2 ▣
Englefield Rd THLE RG7...... 46 A1
Ennerdale Rd WHIT RG2...... 50 C2
Enstone Rd WODY RG5...... 44 D2
Epping Cl READ RG1...... 2 C6
Epsom Ct READ RG1...... 41 F4
Erica Dr EWKG RG40...... 65 E3
Eric Av CAV/SC RG4...... 33 H1
Eriswell Cl EARL RG6...... 52 B3
Erleigh Court Dr EARL RG6...... 43 F3
Erleigh Court Gdns EARL RG6... 43 F3
Erleigh Rd READ RG1...... 3 K7
Eskdale Rd WWKG RG41...... 52 D1
Eskin Cl RDGW RG30...... 40 B3
Essame Cl EWKG RG40...... 65 E2
Essex St WHIT RG2...... 42 A5
Essex Wy CAV/SC RG4...... 23 H1
Ester Carling La HEN RG9...... 13 E1
Eustace Crs EWKG RG40...... 55 F5
Evelyn Ct WODY RG5...... 44 C5
Evendon's Cl WWKG RG41...... 64 B5
Evendon's La WWKG RG41...... 70 B1
Evergreen Dr CALC RG31...... 48 A1 ▣
Evergreen Wy WWKG RG41...... 64 A3 ▣
Eversley Rd WHIT RG2...... 68 B1
Evesham Rd CAV/SC RG4...... 34 A2
Exbourne Rd READ RG2...... 50 B5
Eynsford Cl CAV/SC RG4...... 34 D2 ▣
Eynsham Cl WODY RG5...... 44 B2

F

Faircross Rd RDGW RG30...... 40 D5 ▣
Fairfax Cl CAV/SC RG4...... 34 A5
Fairfield Rd GOR/PANG RG8...... 8 C2
Fairford Rd CALC RG31...... 31 F5
Fair Lawn Gn WHIT RG2...... 51 H5
Fairlop Cl CALC RG31...... 47 G1 ▣
Fairmead Rd WHIT RG2...... 60 D3
Fair Mile HEN RG9...... 5 H2
Fairsted Cl RDGW RG30...... 40 B2 ▣
Fairview Av EARL RG6...... 43 G4
Fairview Rd EWKG RG40...... 64 D3
Fairwater Dr WODY RG5...... 44 A4
Fairway Av RDGW RG30...... 39 G4
Fairway Dr WAR/TWY RG10...... 36 D2 ▣
Fakenham Cl EARL RG6...... 51 F5 ▣
Falcon Av WHIT RG2...... 51 H5
Falcon Wy WWKG RG41...... 64 A2 ▣
Fallowfield Cl CAV/SC RG4...... 34 A3
Falmouth Rd WHIT RG2...... 60 B1
Falstaff Av EARL RG6...... 51 E3
Faraday Cl WHIT RG2...... 68 B4 ▣
Faraday Wy EWKG RG40...... 68 D5
Farleigh Ms CAV/SC RG4...... 34 D2
Farman Cl WODY RG5...... 45 E2
Farm Cl GOR/PANG RG8...... 31 F2
Farm Dr CALC RG31...... 39 E4
Farmers Cl WHIT RG2...... 60 B2 ▣
Farmers End WAR/TWY RG10...... 37 E3
Farm Rd GOR/PANG RG8...... 8 B3
Farnham Dr CAV/SC RG4...... 34 D3
Farnsfield Cl EARL RG6...... 51 F5 ▣
Farriers Cl WODY RG5...... 44 B3
Far Rd HEN RG9...... 16 C1
Farrowdene Rd WHIT RG2...... 50 B5
Fatherson Rd READ RG1...... 3 K6
Fawcett Crs WODY RG5...... 44 A4
Fawley Rd RDGW RG30...... 40 D5
Faygate Wy EARL RG6...... 51 G4
Felixstowe Cl EARL RG6...... 52 A3
The Fells CALC RG31...... 38 D4 ▣
Felstead Cl EARL RG6...... 51 E3
Felthorpe Cl EARL RG6...... 51 F5 ▣
Felton Wy CALC RG31...... 39 F2
Fennel Cl EARL RG6...... 51 E4 ▣
Fernbank EWKG RG40...... 69 G4 ▣
Ferndale Av RDGW RG30...... 48 A1
Ferndale Cl CALC RG31...... 31 H4 ▣
Ferne Cl GOR/PANG RG8...... 8 B2 ▣
Fern Gln CALC RG31...... 39 F1 ▣
Fernhurst Rd CALC RG31...... 47 F1 ▣
Ferry La WAR/TWY RG10...... 27 F2
Fidlers Wk WAR/TWY RG10...... 27 H2
Field Rd READ RG1...... 2 A7
Field Vw CAV/SC RG4...... 34 C2
Fieldway WWKG RG41...... 53 G3 ▣
Filbert Dr CALC RG31...... 39 F2

Filey Rd READ RG1...... 42 D3
Finbeck Wy EARL RG6...... 51 E5
Finchampstead Rd EWKG RG40... 64 C4
  EWKG RG40...... 70 B4 ▣
Finch Rd EARL RG6...... 51 H1
Finch Wy THLE RG7...... 57 E5
Finstock Cl EARL RG6...... 52 A4
Fir Cottage Rd EWKG RG40...... 69 H3 ▣
Fircroft Cl CALC RG31...... 39 F1
Firmstone Cl EARL RG6...... 51 H4
Firs Cl EWKG RG40...... 70 A4
Firs La RDGW RG30...... 41 E5
Firs Rd CALC RG31...... 39 F4
Fishers Ct CAV/SC RG4...... 34 B1
Fishponds Cl WWKG RG41...... 64 B3
Fishponds Rd WWKG RG41...... 64 B4
Fitzroy Crs WODY RG5...... 44 D4
Five Acre CALC RG31...... 39 E1
Flambards CAV/SC RG4...... 34 B5
Flamborough Cl EARL RG6...... 52 B3 ▣
Flamingo Cl WWKG RG41...... 63 H3 ▣
Flaxman Cl EARL RG6...... 51 E3
Fleet Cl WWKG RG41...... 63 H2 ▣
Fleetham Gdns EARL RG6...... 51 G4
Fleming Cl WHIT RG2...... 68 B4
Flodden Dr CALC RG31...... 47 G1 ▣
Florence Wk READ RG1...... 42 C3
Florian Gdns RDGW RG30...... 40 C5 ▣
Flower's Hl GOR/PANG RG8...... 29 H3
Fobney St READ RG1...... 2 E6
Folly Gn GOR/PANG RG8...... 10 B1
Folly La THLE RG7...... 56 C3
Folly Orchard Rd
  GOR/PANG RG8...... 10 B1
Fontwell Dr RDGW RG30...... 40 A5
Forbury Rd READ RG1...... 3 G4
The Forbury READ RG1...... 3 F4
Fordham Wy EARL RG6...... 51 H4 ▣
Forest Dean WHIT RG2...... 60 B1 ▣
Forest Hl RDGW RG30...... 32 A5
Forest Rd EWKG RG40...... 54 D2
  WWKG RG41...... 53 H5
Forge Cl CAV/SC RG4...... 3 J1
Formby Cl EARL RG6...... 52 B2
Forndon Cl EARL RG6...... 52 B3 ▣
Fosters La WODY RG5...... 44 B4
Fowler Cl EARL RG6...... 51 F2
Foxborough THLE RG7...... 66 C5
Fox Cl THLE RG7...... 56 D5
Foxcombe Dr CAV/SC RG4...... 39 F3
Foxcote EWKG RG40...... 70 B4
Foxes Wk WAR/TWY RG10...... 36 D4
Foxglove Cl WWKG RG41...... 63 G1
Foxglove Gdns READ RG1...... 2 A4
Foxhays Rd WHIT RG2...... 50 C5
Foxhill Cl CAV/SC RG4...... 35 F2
Foxhill La CAV/SC RG4...... 24 C5
Foxhill Rd READ RG1...... 42 D4
Foxhunt Gv CALC RG31...... 48 A1 ▣
Framlingham Dr CAV/SC RG4... 34 D2 ▣
Frampton Cl WODY RG5...... 44 B1
Francis St READ RG1...... 42 A4
Franklin St READ RG1...... 2 B6
Fraser Av CAV/SC RG4...... 34 B1
Frederick Pl WWKG RG41...... 64 B2
Freesia Cl WWKG RG41...... 63 G1 ▣
Frensham Gn WHIT RG2...... 51 E4
Freshfield Cl EARL RG6...... 52 B2 ▣
Freshwater Rd READ RG1...... 42 D2
Friar St READ RG1...... 2 D4
Friday St HEN RG9...... 6 B5
Frieth Cl EARL RG6...... 51 F3
Frilsham Rd RDGW RG30...... 48 C1
Frimley Cl WODY RG5...... 44 A2 ▣
Fringford Cl EARL RG6...... 51 H4
Frog Hall Dr EWKG RG40...... 65 F2
Frogmore Wy RDGW RG30...... 40 C5
Froxfield Av READ RG1...... 41 F5
Fuchsia Cl CALC RG31...... 39 F5 ▣
Fullbrook Cl WWKG RG41...... 54 B4
Fullbrook Crs CALC RG31...... 31 G4
Fuller's La THLE RG7...... 58 C4
Fulmead Rd RDGW RG30...... 40 D2
Fulmer Cl EARL RG6...... 51 F5 ▣

G

Gainsborough Cl WODY RG5...... 44 D4 ▣
Gainsborough Crs HEN RG9...... 15 H1
Gainsborough Hl HEN RG9...... 16 A1
Gainsborough Rd HEN RG9...... 15 H1
  RDGW RG30...... 40 C5
Gairn Cl RDGW RG30...... 40 B3
Galsworthy Dr CAV/SC RG4...... 34 C2
Gap Wy GOR/PANG RG8...... 10 C1
Gardeners La GOR/PANG RG8...... 28 B3

Garde Rd CAV/SC RG4...... 36
Garnet Hl READ RG1...... 2
Garnet St READ RG1...... 2
Garrard St READ RG1...... 2
Garrett Rd EWKG RG40...... 64
Garston Cl RDGW RG30...... 48 B▣
Garston Crs CALC RG31...... 39
Garston Gv EWKG RG40...... 70 A▣
Garth Cl WHIT RG2...... 53
Gaskells End CAV/SC RG4...... 23
Gas La WAR/TWY RG10...... 37
Gas Works Rd READ RG1...... 3
Gatcombe Cl CALC RG31...... 47
Gatehampton Rd
  GOR/PANG RG8...... 8
Gayhurst Cl CAV/SC RG4...... 34
Gazelle Cl WWKG RG41...... 52
Gelder Cl EARL RG6...... 52
Geoffreyson Rd CAV/SC RG4...... 33 E2 ▣
George St READ RG1...... 2
Gibbs Cl EWKG RG40...... 69
Gifford Cl CAV/SC RG4...... 34 D2 ▣
Gilbert Wy EWKG RG40...... 69
Gillette Wy WHIT RG2...... 50
Gillotts Cl HEN RG9...... 15
Gillott's La HEN RG9...... 15
Gingells Farm Rd
  WAR/TWY RG10...... 37 E2 ▣
Gipsy La EARL RG6...... 52
  EWKG RG40...... 64
  RDGW RG30...... 39
  WWKG RG41...... 62
The Glade CALC RG31...... 31
Gladridge Cl EARL RG6...... 51 G1 ▣
Glamis Wy CALC RG31...... 47 E▣
Glebe Gdns CAV/SC RG4...... 36
Glebelands Rd EWKG RG40...... 64
Glebe La CALC RG31...... 31
Glebe Ride GOR/PANG RG8...... 8
Glebe Rd GOR/PANG RG8...... 31
  WHIT RG2...... 42
Glenbeigh Ter READ RG1...... 41
Glendevon Rd WODY RG5...... 44
Glennon Cl RDGW RG30...... 48 D▣
Glenrhondda CAV/SC RG4...... 33
Glenrosa Rd RDGW RG30...... 40
Glenwood Dr CALC RG31...... 31
Gloucester Rd RDGW RG30...... 41
Glyncastle CAV/SC RG4...... 34
Goddard Cl WHIT RG2...... 60
Goddard Ct WWKG RG41...... 53 E4 ▣
Godstow Cl WODY RG5...... 44 B2 ▣
Goldcrest Wy CALC RG31...... 47
Goldsmid Rd READ RG1...... 2
Goldsmith Cl EWKG RG40...... 69 H2 ▣
Goldthorpe Gdns EARL RG6...... 51 E5 ▣
Goodchild Rd EWKG RG40...... 65
Goodings Gn EWKG RG40...... 65
Goodliffe Gdns CALC RG31...... 31 F3 ▣
Goodrich Cl CAV/SC RG4...... 34
Goodwin Cl CALC RG31...... 47
Gordon Pl RDGW RG30...... 40
Goring Rd GOR/PANG RG8...... 10
Gorrick Sq WWKG RG41...... 64
Gorse Dr WODY RG5...... 44 D2 ▣
Gorselands CAV/SC RG4...... 33
Gorse Ride North EWKG RG40... 69
Gorse Ride South EWKG RG40... 69
Gosbrook Rd CAV/SC RG4...... 34 B5 ▣
Gosforth Cl EARL RG6...... 52
Gower St READ RG1...... 2
Graffham Cl EARL RG6...... 51 G5 ▣
Grafton Rd RDGW RG30...... 39
Graham Cl CALC RG31...... 47 H1 ▣
Grahame Av GOR/PANG RG8...... 30
Granby Ct READ RG1...... 42
Granby End THLE RG7...... 57 E5 ▣
Granby Gdns EARL RG6...... 42
Grange Av EARL RG6...... 43
  HEN RG9...... 13
Grange Cl GOR/PANG RG8...... 8
Grangely Cl CALC RG31...... 47
Grange Rd HEN RG9...... 6
Grantham Rd CAV/SC RG4...... 23
Granville Rd RDGW RG30...... 40 C5 ▣
Grasmere Av RDGW RG30...... 32
Grasmere Cl WWKG RG41...... 53 E4 ▣
Grass Hl CAV/SC RG4...... 33
Gratton Rd WHIT RG2...... 50 B5
Gratwicke Rd RDGW RG30...... 39
Gravel Hl CAV/SC RG4...... 33
  HEN RG9...... 13
Gravel Hill Crs HEN RG9...... 13
Gravel Rd CAV/SC RG4...... 13
Graveney Dr CAV/SC RG4...... 13
Gravett Cl HEN RG9...... 15
Grays Crs WODY RG5...... 43
Grazeley Rd THLE RG7...... 59

reat Knollys St READ RG1............. 2 B4
reat Lea THLE RG7.................... 59 H3
reen Acre Mt RDCW RG30.......... 39 G2
reenacres Av WWKG RG41........... 52 D3
reenacres La WWKG RG41........... 52 D3
een Cft EWKG RG40.................. 55 F5
een Dean Hl CAV/SC RG4........... 22 C4
een Dr EWKG RG40................... 65 E4
eenfields Rd WHIT RG2.............. 50 A5
eenfield Wy CWTH RG45............ 71 H4
eenfinch Cl CALC RG31.............. 39 E4
een Finch Cl CWTH RG45........... 71 G5
eenham Cl WODY RG5.............. 44 D4
eenidge Cl READ RG30.............. 41 F5
een La CAV/SC RG4.................. 13 G4
 CAV/SC RG4........................ 25 F3
 EWKG RG40......................... 55 H3
 GOR/PANG RG8..................... 10 C2
 GOR/PANG RG8..................... 29 H2
 HEN RG9............................ 16 A1
 RDGW RG30......................... 48 B3
 WAR/TWY RG10..................... 53 H3
 WWKG RG41......................... 53 G4
eenleas CAV/SC RG4................ 24 A5
eenmoor GOR/PANG RG8........... 10 C1
een Rd EARL RG6.................... 43 E5
eensward La WHIT RG2............. 61 H5
he Green WHIT RG2................. 63 H1
eenwood Gv WWKG RG41.......... 53 G2
eenwood Rd CWTH RG45........... 71 H5
 RDGW RG30......................... 40 A5
egory Cl EARL RG6.................. 51 H5
resham Wy RDGW RG30............ 32 B5
reyfriars Rd READ RG1.............. 2 E4
reys Ct READ RG1................... 3 A6
reys Hl HEN RG9.................... 6 C5
reys Rd HEN RG9.................... 15 F1
reystoke Rd CAV/SC RG4........... 34 B3
rimmer Wy GOR/PANG RG8........ 10 C1
rosvenor Rd CAV/SC RG4........... 34 B4
rove Cl EWKG RG40................. 71 F4
rove Hl CAV/SC RG4................. 33 H3
roveland Pl RDGW RG30............ 40 C2
rovelands Av WWKG RG41.......... 53 G3
rovelands Cl WWKG RG41.......... 53 G2
rovelands Rd THLE RG7............. 66 B1
 RDGW RG30......................... 40 C2
rove Rd CAV/SC RG4................ 13 G4
 CAV/SC RG4........................ 33 H2
 HEN RG9............................ 6 B5
he Grove READ RG1................. 3 H6
 WAR/TWY RG10..................... 37 G2
un St READ RG1..................... 2 E5
urney Cl CAV/SC RG4................ 33 E2
urney Dr CAV/SC RG4............... 33 E3
wynne Cl CALC RG31................ 31 G4

H

addon Dr WODY RG5................ 44 B2
adleigh Ri CAV/SC RG4............. 34 D2
afod CAV/SC RG4.................... 33 G1
agbourne Cl GOR/PANG RG8...... 10 C1
agley Rd WHIT RG2................. 50 A1
alcyon Ter RDGW RG30............. 39 H2
aldane Rd CAV/SC RG4............. 33 F2
alfacre Cl THLE RG7................. 60 A5
alls La WHIT RG2.................... 50 D5
alls Rd RDGW RG30................. 39 F4
alpin Cl CALC RG31................. 47 F1
alstead Cl WODY RG5............... 44 B3
ambledon Cl EARL RG6............. 52 B4
amilton Av HEN RG9................ 6 B5
he Hamlet CAV/SC RG4............. 12 C4
ampden Rd CAV/SC RG4............ 34 A5
ampshire Wy WWKG RG41......... 63 G2
anbury Dr CALC RG31............... 47 G1
anningtons Wy THLE RG7........... 57 F5
anwood Cl WODY RG5.............. 43 H2
arcourt Cl READ RG1............... 5 H5
arcourt Dr EARL RG6................ 51 E3
arding Rd WODY RG5............... 43 H2
ardwick Rd GOR/PANG RG8....... 20 A5
 RDGW RG30......................... 40 A3
ardy Cl CAV/SC RG4................. 34 B5
arefield Cl WWKG RG41............. 53 F3
arlech Av CAV/SC RG4.............. 34 D2
arley Rd READ RG1.................. 34 A5
arlton Cl EARL RG6.................. 51 H5
arman Ct WWKG RG41.............. 53 E3
armar Cl EWKG RG40................ 65 F2
arness Cl WHIT RG2................. 60 A2
arpsden Rd HEN RG9............... 16 B1

Harpsden Wy HEN RG9............. 16 B2
Harrier Cl WODY RG5............... 44 D4
Harrington Cl EARL RG6............ 51 H3
Harris Cl WODY RG5................ 45 E2
Harrogate Rd CAV/SC RG4......... 33 F3
Harrow Ct READ RG1............... 2 B7
Hart Dyke Cl WWKG RG41......... 70 C1
Hartigan Pl WODY RG5............. 44 D2
Hartland Rd WHIT RG2............. 50 C4
Hartley Court Rd THLE RG7........ 59 G2
Hartsbourne Rd EARL RG6......... 51 F2
Harts Cl WHIT RG2.................. 68 B1
Hartslock Ct GOR/PANG RG8...... 29 C1
Hartslock Vw GOR/PANG RG8..... 18 D2
Hartslock Wy CALC RG31.......... 31 F3
Hart St READ RG1................... 2 A4
Harvard Cl WODY RG5.............. 45 E2
Harvest Cl CALC RG31.............. 39 E4
Harwich Cl EARL RG6............... 52 A4
Hastings Cl RDGW RG30........... 48 B1
Hatch La RDGW RG30.............. 57 G2
Hatch Ride EWKG RG40............ 71 G3
Hatfield Ct CALC RG31............. 47 E1
Hatford Rd RDGW RG30............ 48 C1
Hatherley Rd READ RG1............ 42 B5
Havelock Rd WWKG RG41.......... 64 B2
Havelock St WWKG RG41........... 64 B2
Hawkchurch Rd WHIT RG2......... 50 C5
Hawkedon Wy EARL RG6........... 52 A3
Hawker Wy WODY RG5............. 44 D4
Hawkesbury Dr CALC RG31........ 47 H2
Hawkes Cl WWKG RG41............ 64 B1
Hawkins Wy EWKG RG40........... 65 F2
Hawksworth Rd THLE RG7......... 57 E5
Hawley Cl CALC RG31.............. 47 F1
Hawthorne Rd CAV/SC RG4....... 34 D4
Hawthornes CALC RG31............ 31 E5
Hawthorn Gdns WHIT RG2......... 50 D3
The Hawthorns WAR/TWY RG10.. 36 D4
Hawthorn Wy CAV/SC RG4........ 36 B5
Hayes La WWKG RG41.............. 63 F4
Hayfield Cl CALC RG31............. 39 F2
Hay Rd READ RG1................... 41 G5
Haywards Cl HEN RG9.............. 5 H5
Haywood Ct EARL RG6............. 43 E3
Haywood Wy RDGW RG30......... 40 A5
Hazelbank EWKG RG40............. 69 C5
Hazel Cl RDGW RG30............... 57 E3
 WWKG RG41......................... 64 A3
Hazel Crs WHIT RG2................ 50 D3
Hazel Dr WODY RG5................ 43 H5
Hazel Gdns CAV/SC RG4........... 13 G3
Hazelmoor La CAV/SC RG4........ 12 D5
Hazel Rd CALC RG31............... 31 F3
Hazelwood Cl CALC RG31.......... 39 F1
Heacham Cl EARL RG6.............. 51 F5
Headington Cl EWKG RG40........ 55 E5
Headington Dr EWKG RG40........ 55 E5
Headley Cl WODY RG5.............. 44 D2
Headley Rd WODY RG5............. 44 D3
Headley Rd East WODY RG5....... 44 D3
Hearn Rd WODY RG5............... 44 B5
Hearns La CAV/SC RG4............. 12 D4
Heath Cl WWKG RG41.............. 64 C4
Heath Dr CAV/SC RG4.............. 25 F3
Heather Cl CAV/SC RG4............ 13 G4
 EWKG RG40......................... 69 H4
Heatherden Cl WHIT RG2.......... 60 B1
Heathermount Dr CWTH RG45.... 71 H5
Heathfield Av HEN RG9............. 25 G2
 RDGW RG30......................... 39 G3
Heathfield Cl HEN RG9............. 25 G2
Heathlands Rd EWKG RG40........ 65 H5
Heath Ride EWKG RG40............ 70 C5
Heath Rd EARL RG6................. 43 F5
Heathway CALC RG31.............. 39 F2
Heelas Rd WWKG RG41............ 64 B3
Helmsdale CALC RG31.............. 40 C2
Helston Gdns WHIT RG2........... 50 A4
Hemdean Hl CAV/SC RG4.......... 33 H4
Hemdean Ri CAV/SC RG4.......... 33 H4
Hemdean Rd CAV/SC RG4......... 33 H3
Hengrave Cl EARL RG6............. 52 B3
Henley Rd CAV/SC RG4............ 34 A4
Henley Wood Rd EARL RG6....... 52 A1
Henry St READ RG1................. 3 F7
Herald Wy CAV/SC RG4............ 44 D4
Hermitage Dr WAR/TWY RG10.... 37 G2
Hermits Cl THLE RG7............... 57 E5
Heroes Wk WHIT RG2............... 60 A1
Heron Dr WAR/TWY RG10......... 37 H1
Heron Island CAV/SC RG4......... 3 H4
Heron Rd WWKG RG41............. 63 H2
Heron Shaw GOR/PANG RG8...... 8 B2
Heron's Wy EWKG RG40........... 65 E1
Heron Wy READ RG1............... 49 F1
Hertford Cl CAV/SC RG4........... 34 C1
 WWKG RG41......................... 63 H3

Hewett Av CAV/SC RG4............ 33 E3
Hewett Cl CAV/SC RG4............. 33 E3
Hexham Rd WHIT RG2.............. 50 B2
Highbridge Cl CAV/SC RG4........ 34 D2
Highbridge Whf READ RG1......... 3 G5
Highbury Rd CALC RG31........... 38 D3
Highcliffe Cl WODY RG5............ 44 C1
Highdown Av CAV/SC RG4......... 33 H1
Highdown Hill Rd CAV/SC RG4.... 23 H5
Highfield EARL RG6................. 51 G3
Highfield Cl EWKG RG40........... 64 C3
Highfield Rd CALC RG31........... 31 E3
Highgate Rd WODY RG5........... 44 A5
Highgrove St READ RG1........... 42 B5
Highgrove Ter READ RG1.......... 42 A4
Highlands Av WWKG RG41......... 63 F3
Highlands La HEN RG9............. 15 F2
Highmead Cl WHIT RG2............ 50 D3
High Meadow CAV/SC RG4........ 33 E4
Highmoor Rd CAV/SC RG4......... 33 G4
High St CAV/SC RG4................ 36 A4
 GOR/PANG RG8..................... 20 A5
 THLE RG7........................... 46 B2
 WAR/TWY RG10..................... 27 C3
 WAR/TWY RG10..................... 37 G2
High Tree Dr EARL RG6............ 43 C4
Highview CALC RG31............... 39 E5
Highworth Wy CALC RG31......... 31 E5
Hilary Cl WHIT RG2................. 60 B1
Hilborn Wy EWKG RG40............ 68 D3
Hilbury Rd EARL RG6............... 51 F2
Hilcot Rd RDGW RG30............. 41 E2
Hildens Dr CALC RG31............. 39 F3
Hill Bottom Cl GOR/PANG RG8... 20 B1
Hillbrow WHIT RG2.................. 50 D4
Hillcrest La HEN RG9............... 13 G2
Hill Lands WAR/TWY RG10........ 27 C2
Hill Rd WHIT RG2................... 68 C2
Hillside GOR/PANG RG8............ 20 A4
 THLE RG7........................... 57 F5
Hillside Pk WHIT RG2............... 51 E4
Hillside Rd EARL RG6............... 52 A2
Hill St READ RG1.................... 42 A4
Hilltop Rd CAV/SC RG4............. 33 E2
 EARL RG6........................... 43 G3
 WAR/TWY RG10..................... 27 H5
Hillview Cl CALC RG31............. 31 E5
Hilmanton EARL RG6............... 51 F5
Hindhead Rd EARL RG6............ 51 F2
Hirstwood RDGW RG30............ 39 H1
Hirtes Av WHIT RG2................ 60 D3
Hocketts Cl GOR/PANG RG8...... 20 B1
Hodsoll Rd READ RG1.............. 2 B3
Hogarth Av RDGW RG30........... 40 B5
Hogwood La EWKG RG40.......... 68 D5
Holberton Rd WHIT RG2............ 50 C5
Holford Cl CALC RG31.............. 39 F2
Holkam Cl RDGW RG30............ 40 A1
Holland Rd RDGW RG30............ 39 G3
Hollicombe Cl RDGW RG30........ 39 H3
Hollow La WHIT RG2................ 60 D3
Hollydale Cl WHIT RG2............. 50 C4
Hollym Cl EARL RG6................ 52 B3
Holly Orch WWKG RG41........... 64 A3
Holly Rd WODY RG5................ 44 D4
Holmbury Av CWTH RG45......... 71 H4
Holmdene THLE RG7................ 57 E5
Holme Cl WHIT RG2................. 71 H4
Holmemoor Dr CAV/SC RG4....... 36 A5
Holme Park Farm La
 CAV/SC RG4........................ 35 H5
Holmes Cl WWKG RG41............ 64 B4
Holmes Crs WWKG RG41........... 64 B4
Holmes Rd EARL RG6............... 43 F5
Holmewood Cl WWKG RG41....... 70 B1
Holmlea Rd GOR/PANG RG8...... 8 B4
Holmwood Av RDGW RG30........ 40 A5
Holsworthy Cl EARL RG6.......... 52 B3
Holt La WWKG RG41................ 64 B1
Holybrook Crs RDGW RG30....... 48 B1
Holybrook Rd READ RG1.......... 41 G5
Holyhook Cl CWTH RG45.......... 71 H5
Holyrood Cl CAV/SC RG4.......... 34 C1
Home Cft CALC RG31............... 39 E1
Home Farm Cl WHIT RG2.......... 60 B3
Homelands Wy HEN RG9.......... 6 A5
Honey End La RDGW RG30........ 40 D5
Honey Hl EWKG RG40.............. 71 G1
Honey Meadow Cl CAV/SC RG4.. 34 D5
Honeysuckle Cl CWTH RG45...... 71 H4
Honiton Rd WHIT RG2.............. 50 C5
Hook End La GOR/PANG RG8..... 18 B3
Hoops Wy WHIT RG2............... 49 G5
Hop Gdns HEN RG9................. 6 A4
Hornbeam Cl GOR/PANG RG8.... 31 F2
 WWKG RG41......................... 63 G5
Hornbeam Dr EARL RG6........... 52 A4
Hornbeams THLE RG7.............. 66 B4

Horncastle Dr RDGW RG30........ 40 A5
Hornsea Cl RDGW RG30........... 39 H1
The Horse Cl CAV/SC RG4......... 34 B3
Horsepond Rd CAV/SC RG4....... 12 C4
Horseshoe Crs THLE RG7.......... 56 D5
Horseshoe Pk GOR/PANG RG8... 30 A2
Horseshoe Rd GOR/PANG RG8... 30 A2
Hose Hl THLE RG7.................. 56 D1
Hosier St READ RG1................ 2 E5
Howard Rd EWKG RG40............ 64 D3
Howard St READ RG1............... 2 C5
Howth Dr WODY RG5............... 44 A3
Huckleberry Cl GOR/PANG RG8.. 31 F3
Hudson Rd WODY RG5............. 44 C5
Hughes Rd EWKG RG40............ 65 E1
Hugh Fraser Dr CALC RG31....... 39 F4
Humber Cl WWKG RG41............ 63 H1
Hungerford Dr READ RG1......... 41 F5
Hunters Cha CAV/SC RG4......... 33 G2
Hunter's Hl THLE RG7.............. 56 C5
Huntingdon Cl EARL RG6.......... 52 B3
Hurricane Wy WODY RG5.......... 44 D3
Hursley Cl RDGW RG30............ 39 H3
Hurst Park Rd WAR/TWY RG10... 37 H5
Hurst Rd WAR/TWY RG10.......... 37 H4
Hurst Wy WHIT RG2................ 49 C5
Huscarle Wy CALC RG31.......... 31 F3
Hutsons Cl EWKG RG40............ 55 E5
Hutton Cl EARL RG6................ 51 F3
Hyde End La THLE RG7............ 60 B4
Hyde End Rd THLE RG7............ 66 A1
The Hydes CALC RG31............. 31 F3
Hyperion Wy WHIT RG2............ 50 A2

I

Ian Mikardo Wy CAV/SC RG4..... 34 C5
Ibstock Cl RDGW RG30............ 40 C3
Ibstone Av CAV/SC RG4............ 34 D2
Icknield Pl GOR/PANG RG8........ 8 C1
Icknield Rd GOR/PANG RG8....... 8 C1
Ilbury Cl WHIT RG2................. 60 D3
Ilchester Ms CAV/SC RG4.......... 34 D1
Ilex Cl CAV/SC RG4................. 13 G5
Ilfracombe Wy EARL RG6.......... 52 B2
Ilkley Rd CAV/SC RG4.............. 33 F4
Illingworth Av CAV/SC RG4........ 34 D1
Ilsley Cl CAV/SC RG4............... 13 G4
Imperial Wy WHIT RG2............. 59 H1
Ingle Gln EWKG RG40.............. 70 B4
Inglewood Cl CAV/SC RG4......... 13 G4
Inglewood Ct RDGW RG30......... 40 D3
Inkpen Cl RDGW RG30............. 48 B1
Instow Rd EARL RG6................ 51 G3
Invergordon Cl CALC RG31........ 47 H1
Irvine Wy EARL RG6................ 51 H5
Isaac Newton Rd WHIT RG2....... 68 C3
Isis Cl WWKG RG41................. 53 E4
Island Rd WHIT RG2................ 49 G2
Ivanhoe Rd EWKG RG40........... 68 D5
Ivybank CALC RG31................. 39 F1
Ivydene Rd RDGW RG30........... 40 D1

J

Jacksons La CAV/SC RG4.......... 32 C2
James's La RDGW RG30............ 57 G4
James St READ RG1................. 2 B5
James Watt Rd EWKG RG40....... 68 D3
Janson Ct READ RG1............... 2 B7
Japonica Cl WWKG RG41.......... 63 G4
Jaques's La THLE RG7.............. 56 C2
Jarvis Dr WAR/TWY RG10......... 37 C1
Jasmine Cl WWKG RG41........... 63 G1
Jay Cl EARL RG6.................... 51 C4
Jefferson Cl CAV/SC RG4.......... 24 B5
Jenkins Cl RDGW RG30............ 40 D4
Jenner Wk CALC RG31............. 38 D3
Jerome Rd WODY RG5............. 44 B5
Jerrymoor Hl EWKG RG40......... 70 A3
Jesse Ter READ RG1................ 2 C6
Joel Cl EARL RG6................... 51 F2
Johnson Dr EWKG RG40........... 70 C4
Jordan Cl CAV/SC RG4............. 34 D2
 THLE RG7........................... 59 F2
Josephine Ct RDGW RG30......... 41 E4
Josey Cl CAV/SC RG4.............. 13 G3
Jubilee Av WWKG RG41............ 64 B1
Jubilee Rd EARL RG6............... 43 F4
Jubilee Sq READ RG1............... 3 G7
Julkes La WHIT RG2................ 62 B1
Junction Rd READ RG1............. 42 D4
The Junipers WWKG RG41......... 63 G4
Juniper Wy CALC RG31............ 31 G5

Jupiter Wy *WWKG* RG41 ... 64 A2
Jutland Cl *WWKG* RG41 ... 63 H2 [10]

K

Katesgrove La *READ* RG1 ... 2 E7
Kathleen Sanders Ct
  THLE RG7 ... 46 B1 [3]
Keane Cl *WODY* RG5 ... 44 B2
Kearsley Rd *RDGW* RG30 ... 40 D4
Keats Cl *WODY* RG5 ... 44 B5
Keats Rd *WODY* RG5 ... 52 B1
Keephatch Rd *EWKG* RG40 ... 55 F5
Kelburne Cl *WWKG* RG41 ... 53 F2
Kelmscott Cl *CAV/SC* RG4 ... 33 F4
Kelsey Av *EWKG* RG40 ... 69 H5
Kelton Cl *EARL* RG6 ... 52 B3
Kelvedon Wy *CAV/SC* RG4 ... 33 F2
Kelvin Cl *WHIT* RG2 ... 68 B4 [2]
Kemble Cl *CALC* RG31 ... 47 G1 [3]
Kemerton Cl *CALC* RG31 ... 47 G1 [2]
Kenavon Dr *READ* RG1 ... 3 H4
Kendal Av *CAV/SC* RG4 ... 34 C2
  WHIT RG2 ... 60 D2 [1]
Kendrick Cl *EWKG* RG40 ... 64 C3
Kendrick Rd *READ* RG1 ... 3 H7
Kenilworth Av *RDGW* RG30 ... 41 E5
Kennedy Dr *GOR/PANG* RG8 ... 30 A2
Kennedy Gdns *EARL* RG6 ... 51 G2
Kennet Ct *WWKG* RG41 ... 64 A2 [6]
Kennet Pl *THLE* RG7 ... 57 E5
Kennet Side *READ* RG1 ... 3 H5
  READ RG1 ... 42 D2
Kennet St *READ* RG1 ... 3 H5
Kennylands Rd *CAV/SC* RG4 ... 13 G5
Kensington Cl *EARL* RG6 ... 51 G4
Kensington Rd *RDGW* RG30 ... 41 E3
Kent Cl *WWKG* RG41 ... 63 G3
Kenton Rd *EARL* RG6 ... 51 H1
Kenton's La *WAR/TWY* RG10 ... 17 G1
Kent Rd *RDGW* RG30 ... 41 E3
Kentwood Cl *RDGW* RG30 ... 39 H1
Kentwood Hl *CALC* RG31 ... 31 H5
  RDGW RG30 ... 39 H1
Kernham Dr *CALC* RG31 ... 31 E5 [2]
Kerris Wy *EARL* RG6 ... 51 F4
Kesteven Wy *WWKG* RG41 ... 63 H2 [11]
Keston Cl *CAV/SC* RG4 ... 34 B4
Kestrel Wy *THLE* RG7 ... 57 E4
  RDGW RG30 ... 48 B1
  WWKG RG41 ... 63 H2
Keswick Cl *RDGW* RG30 ... 39 G3
Keswick Gdns *WODY* RG5 ... 44 B5
Kettering Cl *CALC* RG31 ... 47 H1
Kibblewhite Crs
  WAR/TWY RG10 ... 37 G1 [1]
Kidmore End Rd *CAV/SC* RG4 ... 23 H4
Kidmore La *CAV/SC* RG4 ... 23 E1
Kidmore Rd *CAV/SC* RG4 ... 33 F1
Kilburn Cl *CALC* RG31 ... 47 G1 [10]
Kildare Gdns *CAV/SC* RG4 ... 34 B4
Kiln Hl *THLE* RG7 ... 67 G4
Kiln La *CALC* RG31 ... 38 D2
  HEN RG9 ... 25 H2
Kiln Ride *EWKG* RG40 ... 70 B4
Kiln Ride Extension *EWKG* RG40 ... 70 B5
Kiln Rd *CALC* RG31 ... 24 B5
Kilnsea Dr *EARL* RG6 ... 52 A4
Kiln View *WHIT* RG2 ... 50 C3
Kilowna Cl *WAR/TWY* RG10 ... 36 D3
Kimberley Cl *READ* RG1 ... 41 F5 [1]
Kimpton Cl *WHIT* RG2 ... 50 D5
Kingfisher Cl *WAR/TWY* RG10 ... 37 H4 [1]
Kingfisher Dr *WODY* RG5 ... 43 H4
Kingfisher Pl *READ* RG1 ... 3 G2
King James Wy *HEN* RG9 ... 15 H1
Kingsbridge Rd *WHIT* RG2 ... 50 A3
Kingsdown Cl *EARL* RG6 ... 51 G3 [9]
Kings Farm La *HEN* RG9 ... 14 C3
Kingsford Cl *WODY* RG5 ... 44 D5
Kingsgate St *READ* RG1 ... 42 C3
Kingsley Cl *WAR/TWY* RG10 ... 36 C3
  WHIT RG2 ... 60 A1
King's Meadow Rd *READ* RG1 ... 3 G3
King's Rd *CAV/SC* RG4 ... 34 A5
  HEN RG9 ... 6 A4
  HEN RG9 ... 6 A4
  READ RG1 ... 3 K5
Kingston Gdns *WHIT* RG2 ... 50 B3 [3]
King St *READ* RG1 ... 3 F5
King Street La *WWKG* RG41 ... 53 E4
Kingsway *CAV/SC* RG4 ... 34 D1
Kinson Rd *RDGW* RG30 ... 40 B1
Kirkfell Cl *CALC* RG31 ... 31 F5
Kirkham Cl *CAV/SC* RG4 ... 34 D1
Kirkstall Ct *CALC* RG31 ... 47 G1 [11]

Kirkwood Crs *THLE* RG7 ... 56 C5 [2]
Kirton Cl *RDGW* RG30 ... 40 C3
Kirtons Farm Rd *RDGW* RG30 ... 48 D4
Kittiwake Cl *WODY* RG5 ... 45 E3
Kitwood Dr *EARL* RG6 ... 52 B4
Knappe Cl *HEN* RG9 ... 15 H1
The Knapp *EARL* RG6 ... 51 F1
Knighton Cl *CAV/SC* RG4 ... 33 H4
Knights Wy *CAV/SC* RG4 ... 34 A2
The Knoll *CALC* RG31 ... 31 E5 [3]
Knossington Cl *EARL* RG6 ... 51 H1
Knowle Cl *CAV/SC* RG4 ... 33 E3
Knowle Rd *WODY* RG5 ... 52 B1
Knowsley Rd *CALC* RG31 ... 31 E4
Kybes La *THLE* RG7 ... 59 E4

L

Laburnum Gdns *WHIT* RG2 ... 50 D4
Laburnum Rd *WWKG* RG41 ... 53 F4
Lackmore Gdns *GOR/PANG* RG8 ... 10 C1
Ladbroke Cl *WODY* RG5 ... 44 C4
Lady Jane Ct *CAV/SC* RG4 ... 34 A4
Ladymask Cl *CALC* RG31 ... 48 A1 [2]
Lakeside *EARL* RG6 ... 51 G2
Lalande Cl *WWKG* RG41 ... 63 H2 [12]
Lambeth Ct *RDGW* RG30 ... 40 A3 [1]
Lambfields *THLE* RG7 ... 46 A2 [1]
Lambourne Cl *CALC* RG31 ... 39 G2 [2]
Lambourne Gdns *EARL* RG6 ... 51 H1
Lambourne Rd *CAV/SC* RG4 ... 13 F4
Lambridge La *HEN* RG9 ... 5 G3
Lambridge Wood Rd *HEN* RG9 ... 5 G2
Lamden Wy *THLE* RG7 ... 57 E5
Lamerton Rd *WHIT* RG2 ... 50 A4
Lamorna Crs *CALC* RG31 ... 39 F1
Lanark Cl *WODY* RG5 ... 44 A4
Lancaster Cl *READ* RG1 ... 42 B5
Lancaster Gdns *EARL* RG6 ... 51 G2
Lancing Cl *RDGW* RG30 ... 41 E3
Landen Ct *EWKG* RG40 ... 64 C3
Landrake Crs *READ* RG1 ... 42 B4
Landsend La *WODY* RG5 ... 37 G5
Lane End Cl *WHIT* RG2 ... 60 D2 [2]
Langborough Rd *EWKG* RG40 ... 64 D3
Langdale Gdns *EARL* RG6 ... 51 E3
Langford Cl *CAV/SC* RG4 ... 34 B2
Langhams Wy *WAR/TWY* RG10 ... 27 G2
Langley Common Rd
  EWKG RG40 ... 68 C2
Langley Hl *CALC* RG31 ... 39 F5
Langley Hill Cl *RDGW* RG30 ... 39 F5
Laniver Cl *EARL* RG6 ... 51 G4
Lapwing Cl *CALC* RG31 ... 39 E4
Larch Av *WWKG* RG41 ... 64 B1
Larch Cl *RDGW* RG30 ... 57 E4
Larch Dr *WODY* RG5 ... 44 A5
Larchside Cl *THLE* RG7 ... 66 A1
Larissa Cl *CALC* RG31 ... 39 H1 [5]
Larkes-Meade *EARL* RG6 ... 51 H4 [1]
Larkspur Cl *WWKG* RG41 ... 63 G1
Larkswood Cl *CALC* RG31 ... 31 G4 [5]
Lashbrook Rd *HEN* RG9 ... 17 E5
Latimer Dr *CALC* RG31 ... 47 F1 [6]
Latimer Rd *WWKG* RG41 ... 64 C3
Laud Cl *WHIT* RG2 ... 41 H4
Laud's Cl *HEN* RG9 ... 5 H5
Laud Wy *EWKG* RG40 ... 65 F2
Launceston Av *CAV/SC* RG4 ... 34 D1 [2]
Launcestone Cl *EARL* RG6 ... 51 G3
Laurel Cl *WWKG* RG41 ... 64 A3
Laurel Dr *CALC* RG31 ... 39 E2
The Laurels *GOR/PANG* RG8 ... 30 A2 [1]
Lavenham Dr *WODY* RG5 ... 44 C2
Lawrence Cl *EWKG* RG40 ... 65 E2
Lawrence Rd *RDGW* RG30 ... 40 B2
Lawson Dr *CAV/SC* RG4 ... 33 F2
Laytom Ri *CALC* RG31 ... 31 F4
Lea Cl *RDGW* RG30 ... 48 B2
Lea Rd *CAV/SC* RG4 ... 13 G5
The Lea *EWKG* RG40 ... 70 A3
Leaver Rd *HEN* RG9 ... 5 H5
Ledbury Cl *RDGW* RG30 ... 40 D2 [2]
Ledbury Dr *CALC* RG31 ... 47 G1 [12]
Ledran Cl *EARL* RG6 ... 51 H5 [7]
Leicester Cl *HEN* RG9 ... 6 A3
Leiston Cl *EARL* RG6 ... 52 A4 [1]
Leith Cl *CWTH* RG45 ... 71 H4
Lemart Cl *RDGW* RG30 ... 39 H2 [3]
Leney Cl *EWKG* RG40 ... 55 E5
Lenham Cl *WWKG* RG41 ... 53 G4
Lennox Cl *CALC* RG31 ... 47 F1 [3]
Lennox Rd *EARL* RG6 ... 43 F5
Leopold Wk *READ* RG1 ... 3 K5 [9]

Lesford Rd *READ* RG1 ... 49 F1
Letcombe St *READ* RG1 ... 3 F6
Lexington Gv *WHIT* RG2 ... 60 B2 [3]
Leyburn Cl *WODY* RG5 ... 44 D2
Leyland Gdns *WHIT* RG2 ... 60 D3
Lichfield Cl *EARL* RG6 ... 51 H4
Lidstone Cl *EARL* RG6 ... 52 A4
Liebenrood Rd *RDGW* RG30 ... 40 D4 [3]
Lilac Cl *GOR/PANG* RG8 ... 31 G2 [2]
The Lilacs *WWKG* RG41 ... 63 F5
Lima Ct *READ* RG1 ... 2 B7
Lime Cl *WWKG* RG41 ... 64 A3
Limefield Cl *EARL* RG6 ... 52 B2 [1]
Limetree Rd *GOR/PANG* RG8 ... 8 A3
Limmer Cl *WWKG* RG41 ... 63 F4 [2]
Limmerhill Rd *WWKG* RG41 ... 63 H3
Lincoln Cl *WWKG* RG41 ... 52 D2
Lincoln Gdns *WAR/TWY* RG10 ... 37 G2
Lincoln Rd *WHIT* RG2 ... 50 B1
Lindberg Wy *WODY* RG5 ... 45 E1 [3]
Lind Cl *EARL* RG6 ... 51 G3
Linden Cl *WWKG* RG41 ... 64 A4
Linden Rd *WHIT* RG2 ... 50 B3
  WODY RG5 ... 52 A1
Lindsey Cl *WWKG* RG41 ... 63 H2
Lines Rd *WAR/TWY* RG10 ... 45 H5
Lingholm Cl *RDGW* RG30 ... 40 A5
Links Dr *RDGW* RG30 ... 40 B2 [8]
Link Wy *WHIT* RG2 ... 68 B1
Linnet Cl *CALC* RG31 ... 39 E4
Lismore Cl *WODY* RG5 ... 52 B1
Lister Cl *GOR/PANG* RG8 ... 31 F2
Littington Cl *EARL* RG6 ... 51 H5 [8]
Little Bowden La
  GOR/PANG RG8 ... 29 E2
Littlecote Dr *READ* RG1 ... 41 F4 [1]
Little Croft Rd *GOR/PANG* RG8 ... 8 B4
Little Frith *EWKG* RG40 ... 70 D5
Little Glebe *CAV/SC* RG4 ... 36 B4
Little Heath Rd *CALC* RG31 ... 38 C3
Little Hill Rd *WAR/TWY* RG10 ... 53 G1
Little John's La *RDGW* RG30 ... 40 D2 [3]
Littlejohn's La *RDGW* RG30 ... 41 E1
Little Oak Dr *CALC* RG31 ... 39 F2 [2]
Littlestead Cl *CAV/SC* RG4 ... 34 D1 [3]
Little St *READ* RG1 ... 2 A4
Litton Rd *WHIT* RG2 ... 50 C3
Liverpool Rd *READ* RG1 ... 42 D2
Livery Cl *READ* RG1 ... 3 G6
Livingstone Gdns *WODY* RG5 ... 44 B5
Llewellyn Pk *WAR/TWY* RG10 ... 27 H2
Lock Pl *READ* RG1 ... 3 K5
Lockstile Md *GOR/PANG* RG8 ... 8 B2
Lockstile Wy *GOR/PANG* RG8 ... 8 B3
Loddon Br *EARL* RG6 ... 52 C2
Loddon Bridge Rd *EARL* RG6 ... 52 C1
  WODY RG5 ... 44 C5
Loddon Dr *WAR/TWY* RG10 ... 27 E3
Loddon Hall Rd *WAR/TWY* RG10 ... 37 H2
Lodge Rd *WAR/TWY* RG10 ... 45 H2
Logan Cl *RDGW* RG30 ... 40 A3 [2]
Lomond Av *CAV/SC* RG4 ... 34 D2
London Rd *EARL* RG6 ... 43 G2
  EWKG RG40 ... 65 F2
  READ RG1 ... 3 H7
  WAR/TWY RG10 ... 37 H1
London St *READ* RG1 ... 3 G6
Long Barn La *WHIT* RG2 ... 50 A2
Longdon Rd *WWKG* RG41 ... 53 F4
Longfield Rd *WAR/TWY* RG10 ... 37 H1
Longhurst Cl *CAV/SC* RG4 ... 34 B4
Long La *CALC* RG31 ... 31 E4
Longleat Dr *CALC* RG31 ... 31 E4 [2]
Longmoore Rd *WHIT* RG2 ... 60 C2 [3]
Longridge Cl *RDGW* RG30 ... 40 C3 [2]
Long's Wy *EWKG* RG40 ... 65 F1
Long Toll *GOR/PANG* RG8 ... 10 D4
Longworth Av *CALC* RG31 ... 39 E3
Lorne Pl *READ* RG1 ... 2 A5
Lorne St *READ* RG1 ... 2 A5
Lovatt Cl *CALC* RG31 ... 39 E3
Lovell Cl *HEN* RG9 ... 15 H1
Loverock Rd *RDGW* RG30 ... 40 D1
Love's Cl *THLE* RG7 ... 56 C5
Lower Armour Rd *CALC* RG31 ... 31 G1 [1]
Lower Brook St *READ* RG1 ... 2 E7
Lower Earley Wy *EARL* RG6 ... 51 H5
Lower Earley Wy (North)
  EARL RG6 ... 52 C3
Lower Earley Wy (West)
  WHIT RG2 ... 60 D1
Lower Elmstone Dr *CALC* RG31 ... 39 F1
Lower Field Rd *READ* RG1 ... 41 H4
Lower Henley Rd *CAV/SC* RG4 ... 34 B5
Lower Meadow Rd *WHIT* RG2 ... 50 C3
Lower Mt *READ* RG1 ... 42 B5
Lower Wokingham Rd
  EWKG RG40 ... 71 E5

Lowes Cl *HEN* RG9 ... 17
Lowfield Gn *CAV/SC* RG4 ... 34
Lowfield Rd *CAV/SC* RG4 ... 34
Lowther Cl *WWKG* RG41 ... 54
Lowther Rd *WWKG* RG41 ... 53
Loxwood *EARL* RG6 ... 64
Lucey Cl *CALC* RG31 ... 31 E4
Luckley Pth *EWKG* RG40 ... 64
Luckley Rd *WWKG* RG41 ... 64
Luckley Wd *WWKG* RG41 ... 64
Luckmore Dr *EARL* RG6 ... 51
Luker Av *HEN* RG9 ... 5
Lulworth Rd *WHIT* RG2 ... 50 B5
Lunds Farm Rd *WODY* RG5 ... 44
Lundy La *RDGW* RG30 ... 40
Luscombe Cl *CAV/SC* RG4 ... 34
Lycroft Cl *GOR/PANG* RG8 ... 8
Lydford Rd *READ* RG1 ... 42
Lyefield Ct *CAV/SC* RG4 ... 34
Lyme Gv *CALC* RG31 ... 39
Lymington Ga *CAV/SC* RG4 ... 33
Lyndhurst Rd *GOR/PANG* RG8 ... 8
  RDGW RG30 ... 40
Lynmouth Rd *READ* RG1 ... 2
Lynton Cl *WODY* RG5 ... 43
Lyon Sq *RDGW* RG30 ... 40
Lysander Cl *WODY* RG5 ... 44
Lytham Cl *RDGW* RG30 ... 48 D1
Lytham End *CALC* RG31 ... 31 E4
Lytham Rd *WODY* RG5 ... 44

M

Mace Cl *EARL* RG6 ... 51
Mackay Cl *CALC* RG31 ... 47
Macphail Cl *EWKG* RG40 ... 55
Magill Cl *THLE* RG7 ... 66 A1
Magnolia Wy *WWKG* RG41 ... 64
Magpie Wy *CALC* RG31 ... 39
Maiden Erlegh Dr *EARL* RG6 ... 51
Maidenhead Rd *EWKG* RG40 ... 55
Maiden Pl *EARL* RG6 ... 52
Maitland Rd *READ* RG1 ... 2
Maiwand Gdns *RDGW* RG30 ... 39 G3
Maker Cl *RDGW* RG30 ... 40
Makins Rd *HEN* RG9 ... 15
Maldon Cl *RDGW* RG30 ... 41 E4
Mallard Cl *EARL* RG6 ... 51
  WAR/TWY RG10 ... 37
Mallard Rw *READ* RG1 ... 2
Mallory Av *CAV/SC* RG4 ... 34
Malone Rd *WODY* RG5 ... 44
Maltby Wy *EARL* RG6 ... 51
Malthouse La *READ* RG1 ... 2
Maltings Pl *READ* RG1 ... 2
Malvern Cl *WODY* RG5 ... 44
Malvern Ct *READ* RG1 ... 42
Malvern Wy *WAR/TWY* RG10 ... 27
Managua Cl *CAV/SC* RG4 ... 34
Manchester Rd *READ* RG1 ... 42
Mandeville Cl *RDGW* RG30 ... 40
Manea Cl *EARL* RG6 ... 51 H5
Manners Rd *WODY* RG5 ... 44
Mannock Wy *WODY* RG5 ... 45
Manor Farm La *GOR/PANG* RG8 ... 29
Manor Farm Rd *WHIT* RG2 ... 50
Manor Park Cl *RDGW* RG30 ... 39 F4
  EWKG RG40 ... 69 G5
Manor Park Dr *EWKG* RG40 ... 69 H5
Manor Rd *GOR/PANG* RG8 ... 8
  GOR/PANG RG8 ... 19
  HEN RG9 ... 16
  WWKG RG41 ... 70
Manor Wood Ga *HEN* RG9 ... 16
Mansell Ct *WHIT* RG2 ... 50
Mansfield Rd *READ* RG1 ... 41
  WWKG RG41 ... 64
Man's Hl *THLE* RG7 ... 57
Maple Cl *CAV/SC* RG4 ... 13
  WWKG RG41 ... 53
Maple Ct *GOR/PANG* RG8 ... 8
Mapledene *CAV/SC* RG4 ... 33
Mapledurham Dr
  GOR/PANG RG8 ... 31
Mapledurham Vw *CALC* RG31 ... 31 G5
Maple Gdns *WHIT* RG2 ... 50
Maple La *GOR/PANG* RG8 ... 28
Marathon Cl *WODY* RG5 ... 45
Marchwood Av *CAV/SC* RG4 ... 24
Marefield *EARL* RG6 ... 51
Marfleet Cl *EARL* RG6 ... 52 B3
Margaret Cl *WHIT* RG2 ... 60
Marigold Cl *CWTH* RG45 ... 71
Marino Wy *EWKG* RG40 ... 68
Markby Wy *EARL* RG6 ... 51
Market Pl *HEN* RG9 ... 6

...READ RG1 .... 3 F5
arks Rd *WWKG* RG41 .... 54 B5
arlborough La *READ* RG1 .... 42 C5
arlborough Ct *READ* RG1 .... 41 G4
arlborough Wy *CALC* RG31 .... 47 E1
arling Cl *CALC* RG31 .... 31 F5
arlow Rd *HEN* RG9 .... 6 B3
armion Rd *HEN* RG9 .... 16 B1
arsack St *CAV/SC* RG4 .... 34 B5
arshall Cl *GOR/PANG* RG8 .... 31 C3
arshland Sq *CAV/SC* RG4 .... 34 A2
arten Pl *CALC* RG31 .... 31 E4
artin Cl *WODY* RG5 .... 44 B4
artineau La *WAR/TWY* RG10 .... 45 H1
artins Dr *WWKG* RG41 .... 54 C5
artins St *EARL* RG6 .... 51 H4
aryland *EWKG* RG40 .... 69 G4
ason St *READ* RG1 .... 2 A4
aster Cl *WODY* RG5 .... 45 E2
atlock Rd *CAV/SC* RG4 .... 33 F3
atthewsgreen Rd *WWKG* RG41 .... 54 B5
awbray Cl *EARL* RG6 .... 51 H2
axwell Cl *WODY* RG5 .... 44 B2
ayfair *RDGW* RG30 .... 39 C3
ayfield Cl *CALC* RG31 .... 47 E1
ayfield Dr *CAV/SC* RG4 .... 34 B4
ay Flds *WWKG* RG41 .... 64 C2
e Maying *WHIT* RG2 .... 60 A2
ay Pk *CALC* RG31 .... 47 H1
ays Cl *EARL* RG6 .... 43 C5
ays La *EARL* RG6 .... 43 C5
ays Rd *EWKG* RG40 .... 65 F2
c Carthy Wy *EWKG* RG40 .... 70 A3
crae's Wk *WAR/TWY* RG10 .... 27 C5
cnair Cl *EARL* RG6 .... 51 F4
ead Cl *CALC* RG31 .... 39 E4
ead La *GOR/PANG* RG8 .... 28 B1
eadow *GOR/PANG* RG8 .... 8 B3
eadowcroft Rd *WHIT* RG2 .... 50 A5
ead Rd *EARL* RG6 .... 52 A2
  HEN RG9 .... 6 B5
  READ RG1 .... 2 C2
  WWKG RG41 .... 64 B3
eadowside *CALC* RG31 .... 39 E1
eadowside Rd *GOR/PANG* RG8 .... 30 A2
eadow Vw *WWKG* RG41 .... 53 G2
eadow Wk *WWKG* RG41 .... 64 B2
eadow Wy *THLE* RG7 .... 46 A2
  WWKG RG41 .... 64 B3
he Meadway *RDGW* RG30 .... 39 H3
e Mearings *RDGW* RG30 .... 57 H4
easham Wy *EARL* RG6 .... 51 H4
eavy Gdns *WHIT* RG2 .... 50 A3
edill Cl *GOR/PANG* RG8 .... 10 B1
edina Cl *WWKG* RG41 .... 63 H2
edlbourne Av *WWKG* RG41 .... 53 F4
edway Cl *WWKG* RG41 .... 64 A1
eldreth Wy *EARL* RG6 .... 51 H4
elford Gn *CAV/SC* RG4 .... 34 D1
elksham Cl *EARL* RG6 .... 50 D5
elling Cl *EARL* RG6 .... 52 B2
elody Cl *WWKG* RG41 .... 53 F2
elrose Av *EARL* RG6 .... 43 F5
elrose Gdns *WHIT* RG2 .... 68 B1
emorial Av *HEN* RG9 .... 26 B2
endip Cl *WAR/TWY* RG10 .... 37 E3
endip Dr *CALC* RG31 .... 38 D4
enpes Rd *CALC* RG31 .... 31 F3
erchants Pl *READ* RG1 .... 2 E4
ercury Av *WWKG* RG41 .... 63 H2
ereoak La *THLE* RG7 .... 59 F5
ermaid Cl *WWKG* RG41 .... 53 E3
errivale Gdns *WHIT* RG2 .... 50 A4
erryhild Green La
  WWKG RG41 .... 53 G2
erryman Dr *CWTH* RG45 .... 71 C5
erryweather Cl *EWKG* RG40 .... 70 A2
erthyr V *CAV/SC* RG4 .... 33 H1
erton Rd North *WHIT* RG2 .... 50 A4
erton Rd South *WHIT* RG2 .... 50 A4
eteor Cl *WODY* RG5 .... 44 D3
e Mews *READ* RG1 .... 42 D4
icklands Rd *CAV/SC* RG4 .... 34 C3
iddlefields *WAR/TWY* RG10 .... 37 H1
idsummer Meadow
  CAV/SC RG4 .... 33 G1
idwinter Cl *RDGW* RG30 .... 39 H2
ilestone Av *WAR/TWY* RG10 .... 36 D3
ilestone Crs *WAR/TWY* RG10 .... 36 D3
iles Wy *WODY* RG5 .... 44 D3
illbank *CALC* RG31 .... 44 C4
ill Cl *WWKG* RG41 .... 64 A1
illdown Av *GOR/PANG* RG8 .... 8 B2
illdown Rd *GOR/PANG* RG8 .... 8 B2
illers Cl *GOR/PANG* RG8 .... 8 B2
illers Gv *CALC* RG31 .... 47 H1
ilford Rd *READ* RG1 .... 2 C2
ll Gn *CAV/SC* RG4 .... 3 J1

Mill La *CALC* RG31 .... 47 H1
  CAV/SC RG4 .... 22 D3
  EARL RG6 .... 52 B5
  HEN RG9 .... 16 C1
  HEN RG9 .... 26 D2
  READ RG1 .... 3 F6
  WWKG RG41 .... 52 D5
Millmead *WWKG* RG41 .... 64 B1
Mill Rd *CAV/SC* RG4 .... 3 H1
  GOR/PANG RG8 .... 9 H6
  HEN RG9 .... 27 E1
  RDGW RG30 .... 47 H3
Millworth La *WHIT* RG2 .... 60 D4
Milman Rd *WHIT* RG2 .... 42 A5
Milsom Cl *WHIT* RG2 .... 60 D3
Milton Cl *HEN* RG9 .... 6 A4
Milton Ct *EWKG* RG40 .... 64 C1
Milton Dr *EWKG* RG40 .... 64 C1
Milton Gdns *EWKG* RG40 .... 64 C1
Milton Rd *EARL* RG6 .... 43 F3
  EWKG RG40 .... 64 C1
  WWKG RG41 .... 64 C1
Minden Cl *WWKG* RG41 .... 63 H2
Minster St *READ* RG1 .... 2 E5
Mint Cl *EARL* RG6 .... 51 E4
Minton Cl *RDGW* RG30 .... 40 A2
Mitcham Cl *WHIT* RG2 .... 42 A5
Mitchell Wy *WODY* RG5 .... 44 D3
Mitford Cl *WHIT* RG2 .... 50 C5
Modbury Gdns *WHIT* RG2 .... 50 B3
Mohawk Wy *WODY* RG5 .... 45 E3
Mole Rd *WHIT* RG2 .... 62 C3
  WWKG RG41 .... 52 D5
Moles Cl *EWKG* RG40 .... 65 E3
Mollison Cl *WODY* RG5 .... 45 E2
Molly Millar Br *WWKG* RG41 .... 64 C4
Molly Millar's La *WWKG* RG41 .... 64 B3
Monksbarn *WHIT* RG2 .... 50 C3
Monkshood Cl *EWKG* RG40 .... 65 F1
Monks Wy *RDGW* RG30 .... 41 E5
Mons Cl *WWKG* RG41 .... 63 H2
Montague Cl *EWKG* RG40 .... 65 F1
Montague St *CAV/SC* RG4 .... 34 B5
  READ RG1 .... 3 K6
Montgomery Dr *THLE* RG7 .... 66 A1
Montpelier Dr *CAV/SC* RG4 .... 34 D2
Moor Cl *EWKG* RG40 .... 69 H4
Moor Copse Cl *EARL* RG6 .... 51 G2
Moores Gn *EWKG* RG40 .... 55 F5
Moorhen Dr *EARL* RG6 .... 51 G4
The Moors *GOR/PANG* RG8 .... 30 A2
Morecambe Av *CAV/SC* RG4 .... 33 F2
Moreleigh Cl *WHIT* RG2 .... 50 B5
Morgan Rd *READ* RG1 .... 42 B5
Moriston Cl *RDGW* RG30 .... 40 C2
Morlais *CAV/SC* RG4 .... 33 C2
Morlands Av *RDGW* RG30 .... 40 B5
Mornington Av *EWKG* RG40 .... 70 A3
Morpeth Cl *WHIT* RG2 .... 50 B2
Mortimer La *WHIT* RG2 .... 50 B2
Moss Cl *CAV/SC* RG4 .... 34 C2
Mountfield *GOR/PANG* RG8 .... 8 B2
Mount Pleasant *WWKG* RG41 .... 64 B2
Mount Pleasant Gv *READ* RG1 .... 42 A4
Mount St *WHIT* RG2 .... 42 A5
The Mount *CAV/SC* RG4 .... 33 C4
  READ RG1 .... 42 C5
Mount Vw *READ* RG1 .... 6 A3
Mowbray Dr *RDGW* RG30 .... 40 B2
Mower Cl *EARL* RG6 .... 65 G1
Muirfield Cl *READ* RG1 .... 3 K6
Mulberry Cl *WODY* RG5 .... 44 B4
Mulberry Wy *THLE* RG7 .... 46 B3
Mumbery Hl *WAR/TWY* RG10 .... 27 H3
Mundesley St *READ* RG1 .... 3 F7
Munro Av *WODY* RG5 .... 52 C1
Murdoch Rd *EWKG* RG40 .... 64 C3
Murray Rd *WHIT* RG2 .... 64 B2
Mustard La *CAV/SC* RG4 .... 44 B1
Muswell Cl *THLE* RG7 .... 46 B2
Mylne Sq *EWKG* RG40 .... 65 E2
Mylum Cl *WHIT* RG2 .... 60 B2
Myrtle Cl *CALC* RG31 .... 31 F4
  THLE RG7 .... 57 F5
Myton Wk *THLE* RG7 .... 46 B2

N

Nabbs Hill Cl *CALC* RG31 .... 39 F5
Napier Rd *READ* RG1 .... 3 G3
Narromine Dr *CALC* RG31 .... 48 A1
Nash Cl *EARL* RG6 .... 51 F2
Nash Grove La *EWKG* RG40 .... 69 H1
The Naylors *THLE* RG7 .... 66 C5
Neath Gdns *RDGW* RG30 .... 40 A3
Nelson Rd *CAV/SC* RG4 .... 34 B5

Neptune Cl *WWKG* RG41 .... 63 H2
Netley Cl *CAV/SC* RG4 .... 34 D1
Nevis Rd *CALC* RG31 .... 31 G4
Newalls Ri *WAR/TWY* RG10 .... 27 H2
Newark St *READ* RG1 .... 3 G7
New Bath Rd *WAR/TWY* RG10 .... 36 D3
Newbery Cl *CALC* RG31 .... 39 G1
New Bright St *READ* RG1 .... 2 E7
Newbury Cl *WAR/TWY* RG10 .... 37 E3
Newcastle Rd *WHIT* RG2 .... 50 B1
Newell's La *CAV/SC* RG4 .... 22 C5
Newfield Rd *CAV/SC* RG4 .... 13 G3
New Hl *GOR/PANG* RG8 .... 31 F2
Newlands Av *CAV/SC* RG4 .... 34 A4
New Lane Hl *RDGW* RG30 .... 39 H4
Newlyn Gdns *WHIT* RG2 .... 50 A4
Newmarket Cl *EARL* RG6 .... 52 A3
Newport Rd *READ* RG1 .... 2 D1
New Rd *HEN* RG9 .... 26 D1
  READ RG1 .... 42 C5
  WAR/TWY RG10 .... 27 G5
  WWKG RG41 .... 52 D5
New St *HEN* RG9 .... 6 B4
Newton Av *CAV/SC* RG4 .... 34 C2
Newtown Gdns *HEN* RG9 .... 16 B1
Newtown Rd *HEN* RG9 .... 16 C1
New Wokingham Rd
  CWTH RG45 .... 71 H5
Niagara Rd *HEN* RG9 .... 16 B1
Nicholas Rd *HEN* RG9 .... 15 G1
Nightingale Rd *WODY* RG5 .... 52 A1
Nimrod Cl *WODY* RG5 .... 44 D3
Nimrod Wy *WHIT* RG2 .... 42 A5
Nine Mile Ride *EWKG* RG40 .... 69 A5
Nire Rd *CAV/SC* RG4 .... 34 D4
Norcot Rd *RDGW* RG30 .... 39 D4
Nores Rd *WHIT* RG2 .... 60 C1
Norfolk Cl *WWKG* RG41 .... 63 H2
Norfolk Rd *RDGW* RG30 .... 40 D3
Norman Av *HEN* RG9 .... 6 B5
Norman Pl *READ* RG1 .... 3 F5
Norman Rd *CAV/SC* RG4 .... 34 B3
Normanstead Rd *CALC* RG31 .... 39 F2
Norreys Av *EWKG* RG40 .... 65 E1
Norris Rd *EARL* RG6 .... 43 E4
Northam Cl *EARL* RG6 .... 52 B2
Northbourne Cl *EARL* RG6 .... 51 G4
Northbrook Rd *CAV/SC* RG4 .... 34 B3
Northbury Av *WAR/TWY* RG10 .... 37 H2
Northbury La *WAR/TWY* RG10 .... 37 H2
Northcourt Av *WHIT* RG2 .... 50 C1
North Dr *THLE* RG7 .... 56 A1
Northfield Cl *HEN* RG9 .... 16 D5
Northfield End *HEN* RG9 .... 6 A3
Northfield Rd *HEN* RG9 .... 17 E5
  READ RG1 .... 2 D2
North St *CAV/SC* RG4 .... 34 A5
  READ RG1 .... 2 C4
Northumberland Av *WHIT* RG2 .... 50 B3
North Wk *THLE* RG7 .... 46 B1
Northway *WWKG* RG41 .... 63 G1
Norton Rd *EWKG* RG40 .... 64 D1
  READ RG1 .... 42 D3
  WODY RG5 .... 44 C5
Norwich Dr *WODY* RG5 .... 43 H2
Norwood Rd *READ* RG1 .... 42 C3
Notton Wy *EARL* RG6 .... 51 E5
Nuffield Rd *WHIT* RG2 .... 68 C4
Nunhide La *GOR/PANG* RG8 .... 38 C1
Nun's Acre *GOR/PANG* RG8 .... 8 A2
Nursery Cl *HEN* RG9 .... 16 D5
  WAR/TWY RG10 .... 45 H2
Nursery Gdns *GOR/PANG* RG8 .... 31 E2
Nuthatch Dr *EARL* RG6 .... 51 G1
Nutmeg Cl *EARL* RG6 .... 51 E4
Nutter's La *WHIT* RG2 .... 67 F2

O

Oakdale Cl *CALC* RG31 .... 39 F2
Oakdene *GOR/PANG* RG8 .... 10 C2
  THLE RG7 .... 56 D5
Oakdown Cl *GOR/PANG* RG8 .... 20 B1
Oak Dr *WODY* RG5 .... 44 D4
Oakham Cl *CALC* RG31 .... 31 G5
Oaklands Dr *WWKG* RG41 .... 64 B4
Oaklands La *CWTH* RG45 .... 71 H5
Oaklands Pk *WWKG* RG41 .... 64 B4
Oakley Rd *CAV/SC* RG4 .... 33 G3
Oakside Wy *WHIT* RG2 .... 50 D5
Oaks Rd *HEN* RG9 .... 16 D5
Oak Tree Copse *CALC* RG31 .... 31 H4
Oak Tree Rd *CALC* RG31 .... 31 G2
Oak Tree Wk *GOR/PANG* RG8 .... 31 G2
Oak Vw *CALC* RG31 .... 39 F2
Oak Wy *WODY* RG5 .... 52 A1

Oatlands Rd *WHIT* RG2 .... 61 E4
Oban Gdns *WODY* RG5 .... 52 B1
Odell Cl *EARL* RG6 .... 51 G5
Odiham Av *CAV/SC* RG4 .... 34 D2
Ogmore Cl *RDGW* RG30 .... 39 H3
Old Acre La *WAR/TWY* RG10 .... 37 E2
Old Barn Cl *CAV/SC* RG4 .... 33 H1
Old Bath Rd *CAV/SC* RG4 .... 36 B5
  CAV/SC RG4 .... 43 H1
  WAR/TWY RG10 .... 36 D3
Old Copse Gdns *HEN* RG9 .... 13 G3
Old Elm Dr *RDGW* RG30 .... 39 G2
Old Farm Crs *CALC* RG31 .... 31 F5
Oldfield Cl *EARL* RG6 .... 43 F4
Old Forest Wk *WWKG* RG41 .... 54 B3
The Old La *READ* RG1 .... 41 G5
Old Mill La *WAR/TWY* RG10 .... 37 G2
The Old Orch *CALC* RG31 .... 47 H1
Old Whitley Wood La *WHIT* RG2 .... 60 B2
Old Wooosehill La *WWKG* RG41 .... 64 A1
Oleander Cl *CWTH* RG45 .... 71 G4
Oliver Dr *CALC* RG31 .... 39 E5
Omer's Ri *THLE* RG7 .... 56 D5
Onslow Gdns *CAV/SC* RG4 .... 34 B4
Opal Wy *WWKG* RG41 .... 63 H1
Oracle Pkwy *EARL* RG6 .... 43 E2
Orbit Cl *EWKG* RG40 .... 70 A5
Orchard Av *CAV/SC* RG4 .... 13 F4
Orchard Cl *CALC* RG31 .... 31 E3
  EWKG RG40 .... 65 E2
  HEN RG9 .... 6 B5
  HEN RG9 .... 26 B2
  THLE RG7 .... 66 A1
Orchard Coombe
  GOR/PANG RG8 .... 20 A1
Orchard Est *WAR/TWY* RG10 .... 37 H2
Orchard Fld *CAV/SC* RG4 .... 12 D4
Orchard Gv *CAV/SC* RG4 .... 34 D3
Orchard Pl *EWKG* RG40 .... 64 D2
Orchard St *READ* RG1 .... 2 E7
The Orchard *THLE* RG7 .... 46 B1
Oregon Av *CALC* RG31 .... 31 F4
Oregon Wk *EWKG* RG40 .... 69 G4
Orkney Cl *CALC* RG31 .... 47 H1
Ormonde Rd *WWKG* RG41 .... 64 B3
Ormsby St *READ* RG1 .... 2 A5
Orrin Cl *RDGW* RG30 .... 40 B2
Orts Rd *READ* RG1 .... 3 J5
  READ RG1 .... 42 C3
Orville Cl *WODY* RG5 .... 44 D3
Orwell Cl *CAV/SC* RG4 .... 33 G3
Osborne Rd *EWKG* RG40 .... 64 D2
  RDGW RG30 .... 40 C2
Osterley Cl *EWKG* RG40 .... 65 G3
Osterley Dr *CAV/SC* RG4 .... 34 D1
Otter Cl *CWTH* RG45 .... 71 H4
Overbury Av *WWKG* RG41 .... 54 A4
Overdown Rd *CALC* RG31 .... 39 F1
Overlanders End *CALC* RG31 .... 31 H4
Owl Cl *WWKG* RG41 .... 63 H3
Owston *EARL* RG6 .... 51 H3
Oxford Rd *CALC* RG31 .... 31 G3
  READ RG1 .... 2 B5
  RDGW RG30 .... 40 C2
  WWKG RG41 .... 64 B2
Oxford St *CAV/SC* RG4 .... 33 H5

P

Pack & Prime La *HEN* RG9 .... 5 H4
Packman Dr *WAR/TWY* RG10 .... 37 G1
Paddick Cl *CAV/SC* RG4 .... 36 B4
Paddick Dr *EARL* 52 A4
Paddock Hts *WAR/TWY* RG10 .... 37 H3
The Paddock *CWTH* RG45 .... 71 H5
Padstow Gdns *READ* RG1 .... 50 A4
Page's Cft *EWKG* RG40 .... 65 E3
Pages Orch *CAV/SC* RG4 .... 13 F4
Paice Gn *EWKG* RG40 .... 65 E1
Palmera Av *CALC* RG31 .... 47 F1
Palmer Cl *EWKG* RG40 .... 71 H3
Palmer Park Av *EARL* RG6 .... 43 E4
Palmer School Rd *EWKG* RG40 .... 64 D2
Palmer's La *THLE* RG7 .... 58 B5
Palmerstone Rd *EARL* RG6 .... 43 F3
Pangbourne Hl *GOR/PANG* RG8 .... 29 F2
Pangbourne Rd *GOR/PANG* RG8 .... 28 D3
Pangbourne St *RDGW* RG30 .... 40 C2
Paprika Cl *EARL* RG6 .... 51 E4
The Parade *WODY* RG5 .... 44 C2
Paradise Rd *HEN* RG9 .... 5 H5
Park Cl *CAV/SC* RG4 .... 13 H3
Parkcorner La *WHIT* RG2 .... 62 C2
Park Crs *RDGW* RG30 .... 40 B4
Parkhill Dr *CALC* RG31 .... 31 G5

Parkhouse La RDGW RG30 .... 41 E4 🔲
Park La CALC RG31 .... 39 F4
   GOR/PANG RG8 .... 11 H3
   WAR/TWY RG10 .... 37 E4
Park Rd EWKG RG40 .... 64 C2
   HEN RG9 .... 6 B5
Parkside HEN RG9 .... 5 H4
Parkside Rd RDGW RG30 .... 41 E4
Park View Dr North
   WAR/TWY RG10 .... 36 D1
Park View Dr South
   WAR/TWY RG10 .... 36 D2
Park Wk GOR/PANG RG8 .... 31 G2 🔲
Park Wall La GOR/PANG RG8 ..... 18 C3
Parkway Dr CAV/SC RG4 .... 36 A4
Parsley Cl EARL RG6 .... 51 E4
Parsons Cl WHIT RG2 .... 68 D4
Parthia Cl READ RG1 .... 2 E7
Partridge Dr CALC RG31 .... 39 E4
Pasture Cl EARL RG6 .... 51 G5
Patriot Pl READ RG1 .... 3 J5
Patten Ash Dr EWKG RG40 .... 65 F1
Pattinson Rd WHIT RG2 .... 60 C2 🔲
Pavenham Cl EARL RG6 .... 51 F5
Payley Dr EWKG RG40 .... 55 F5
Peach St EWKG RG40 .... 64 D2
Pearce's Orch HEN RG9 .... 6 A4
Pearson Rd CAV/SC RG4 .... 36 A4
Pearson Wy WODY RG5 .... 44 B5
Peel Cl CAV/SC RG4 .... 34 C5
Pegasus Cl CALC RG31 .... 39 F3 🔲
Peg's Gn RDGW RG30 .... 40 C3 🔲
Peg's Green Cl RDGW RG30 ...... 40 C4 🔲
Pell St READ RG1 .... 42 A4
Pemberton Gdns CALC RG31 ..... 47 G1
Pembroke Cl THLE RG7 .... 57 F5
Pembroke Pl CAV/SC RG4 .... 34 B4
Pendennis Av CAV/SC RG4 .... 34 D1
Pendred Rd WHIT RG2 .... 60 B2
Penn Cl CAV/SC RG4 .... 33 H1
Pennfields WAR/TWY RG10 ...... 37 H1
Pennine Cl CALC RG31 .... 39 E4 🔲
Pennine Wy WAR/TWY RG10 .... 37 E3
Pennypiece GOR/PANG RG8 .... 8 B2
Penroath Av RDGW RG30 .... 40 D4
Penrose Av WODY RG5 .... 44 B4
Pentland Cl RDGW RG30 .... 40 A5 🔲
Peppard Hl HEN RG9 .... 13 C1
Peppard La HEN RG9 .... 16 A2
Peppard Rd CAV/SC RG4 .... 24 B5
   CAV/SC RG4 .... 34 A3
   CAV/SC RG4 .... 34 B3
Pepper La EARL RG6 .... 50 D1
Peregrine Cl WWKG RG41 .... 64 A3 🔲
Periam Cl HEN RG9 .... 15 H1
Perkins Wy WWKG RG41 .... 64 B3
Perseverance Hl HEN RG9 .... 15 F4
Perth Cl WODY RG5 .... 44 D1
Petrel Cl WWKG RG41 .... 63 H3 🔲
Petworth Av CALC RG31 .... 48 A2 🔲
Pevensey Av CAV/SC RG4 .... 34 D2
Pheasant Cl WWKG RG41 .... 53 F4
Phillimore Rd CAV/SC RG4 .... 24 B4
Phillips Cl WODY RG5 .... 45 E1
Phoenix Vil WWKG RG41 .... 63 H2 🔲
Phyllis Court Dr HEN RG9 .... 6 B3
Picketts La GOR/PANG RG8 ...... 28 D3
Pickwell Cl EARL RG6 .... 51 H4
Picton Wy CAV/SC RG4 .... 34 A3
Piercefield CALC RG31 .... 47 E1
Pierce's Hl CALC RG31 .... 39 F1
Piggott's Rd CAV/SC RG4 .... 3 J1
Pigott Rd EWKG RG40 .... 55 E5
Pikeshaw Wy CALC RG31 .... 31 F5 🔲
Pimento Dr EARL RG6 .... 51 E4
Pincents La CALC RG31 .... 46 D1
   THLE RG7 .... 38 D5
Pinchcut THLE RG7 .... 56 D5
Pine Croft Rd WWKG RG41 .... 70 B1
Pine Dr EWKG RG40 .... 70 B4
Pine Gv WAR/TWY RG10 .... 37 G2
Pine Ridge Rd THLE RG7 .... 56 D5
The Pines WAR/TWY RG10 .... 27 H5
Pinetree Cl CAV/SC RG4 .... 33 H2 🔲
Pingewood Rd RDGW RG30 ...... 48 B4 🔲
Pingewood Rd North
   RDGW RG30 .... 48 B3
Pingewood Rd South
   RDGW RG30 .... 58 C1
Pitcroft Av EARL RG6 .... 43 F4
Pitford Rd WODY RG5 .... 44 C2
Pitt's La EARL RG6 .... 43 G3
Players Gn WODY RG5 .... 44 B5 🔲
Playhatch Rd CAV/SC RG4 .... 35 F2
Play Platt THLE RG7 .... 46 A1
Plough La EWKG RG40 .... 65 G1
   HEN RG9 .... 26 B3
Plover Cl WWKG RG41 .... 64 A3 🔲

Plowden Wy HEN RG9 .... 26 B3
Plumtrees EARL RG6 .... 51 G3
Plymouth Av WODY RG5 .... 43 H5
Plympton Cl EARL RG6 .... 52 B2
Polehampton Cl
   WAR/TWY RG10 .... 37 G3
Pollards Wy CALC RG31 .... 47 F1
Polsted Rd CALC RG31 .... 39 G1
Pond End Rd CAV/SC RG4 .... 13 H3
Pond Head La WODY RG5 .... 52 A1
Pond La CAV/SC RG4 .... 32 A1
Poole Cl RDGW RG30 .... 40 A3
Poplar Av RDGW RG30 .... 40 A5 🔲
Poplar Gdns WHIT RG2 .... 50 D4
Poplar La WWKG RG41 .... 53 G2
Poppy Pl EWKG RG40 .... 64 C2
Poppy Wy CALC RG31 .... 39 F5
Porchfield Cl EARL RG6 .... 51 F4
Porlock Pl CALC RG31 .... 47 F1 🔲
Porter Cl EARL RG6 .... 51 H5 🔲
Portland Gdns RDGW RG30 ...... 39 F3
Portman Rd RDGW RG30 .... 40 C1
Portmeirion Gdns RDGW RG30 .. 40 A1 🔲
Portrush Cl WODY RG5 .... 44 A4
Portway Cl READ RG1 .... 41 F4
Post Horn Pl CALC RG31 .... 48 A1 🔲
Post Office La RDGW RG30 .... 57 F3
Potkiln La GOR/PANG RG8 .... 10 B3
Pottery Rd RDGW RG30 .... 39 H1
Pound La CAV/SC RG4 .... 36 B5
Preston Rd WHIT RG2 .... 42 A5
Priest Av EWKG RG40 .... 65 G3
Priest Hl CAV/SC RG4 .... 33 H4
Primrose Cl CAV/SC RG4 .... 34 C5
Primrose La WWKG RG41 .... 53 F2
Prince of Wales Av RDGW RG30 .. 41 E3
Princess Marina Dr EWKG RG40.. 68 D2
   WHIT RG2 .... 68 C3
Prince's St READ RG1 .... 3 J6
Prince William Dr CALC RG31 ...... 39 F1
Prior's Ct READ RG1 .... 3 F7
Priory Av CAV/SC RG4 .... 33 H5
Priory Cl WWKG RG41 .... 53 F5
The Priory WWKG RG41 .... 53 F2 🔲
Privet Cl EARL RG6 .... 51 G4
Proctors Rd EWKG RG40 .... 65 G2
Promenade Rd READ RG1 .... 33 H5
Prospect St CAV/SC RG4 .... 33 H5
   READ RG1 .... 2 A6
Purfield Dr WAR/TWY RG10 ...... 27 H2
Purley La GOR/PANG RG8 .... 31 F2
Purley Ri GOR/PANG RG8 .... 30 C2
Purley Village GOR/PANG RG8 .... 31 F2
Purley Wy GOR/PANG RG8 .... 30 B2
Pursers Farm THLE RG7 .... 60 A5 🔲
Purslane EWKG RG40 .... 65 E3

Q

Quantock Av CAV/SC RG4 .... 34 C2
Quantock Cl WAR/TWY RG10 ...... 37 E3 🔲
Quarry La HEN RG9 .... 16 D5
Quartz Cl WWKG RG41 .... 63 G1
Queen Annes Ga CAV/SC RG4 .... 34 B4
Queen Cl HEN RG9 .... 6 B5
Queensborough Dr CAV/SC RG4 .. 33 F2
Queen's Cottages READ RG1 ...... 3 G5
The Queen's Dr EARL RG6 .... 50 C1
Queens Ride CWTH RG45 .... 71 H4
Queen's Rd CAV/SC RG4 .... 3 H1
   READ RG1 .... 3 G6
Queen St CAV/SC RG4 .... 33 H4
   HEN RG9 .... 6 B5
Queensway CAV/SC RG4 .... 34 C1
Queen Victoria St READ RG1 ...... 3 F5
Quentin Rd WODY RG5 .... 44 A4

R

Radbourne Rd CALC RG31 .... 47 G1
Radcot Cl WODY RG5 .... 44 B1
Radical Ride EWKG RG40 .... 70 A4
Radnor Cl HEN RG9 .... 6 B4
Radnor Rd EARL RG6 .... 51 H2
Radstock La EARL RG6 .... 51 F2
Radstock Rd READ RG1 .... 43 E3
Ragdale THLE RG7 .... 56 D5
Raggleswood Cl EARL RG6 .... 51 H2 🔲
Raglan Gdns CAV/SC RG4 .... 34 B3
Ragley Ms CAV/SC RG4 .... 34 C1 🔲
Railton Cl WHIT RG2 .... 60 C1 🔲
Rainbow Pk WWKG RG41 .... 53 E3
Rainworth Cl EARL RG6 .... 51 F5 🔲
Raleigh Cl WODY RG5 .... 44 B5

Ramsbury Dr EARL RG6 .... 51 F1
Ramsey Cl EARL RG6 .... 52 B3
Rances La EWKG RG40 .... 65 F2
Randolph Rd READ RG1 .... 2 D1
Range Rd EWKG RG40 .... 70 C4
Rangewood Av CALC RG31 .... 48 A2
Ratby Cl EARL RG6 .... 51 H3
Ravenglass Cl EARL RG6 .... 51 H3
Ravensbourne Dr WODY RG5 ...... 44 B2
Ravenscroft Rd HEN RG9 .... 6 A4
Reade's La CAV/SC RG4 .... 12 D4
Reading Rd CAV/SC RG4 .... 12 A5
   GOR/PANG RG8 .... 8 C3
   GOR/PANG RG8 .... 29 C1
   HEN RG9 .... 16 B1
   RDGW RG30 .... 57 F4
   WHIT RG2 .... 61 H4
   WODY RG5 .... 44 A2
   WWKG RG41 .... 53 E3
   WWKG RG41 .... 64 B1
Recreation La THLE RG7 .... 66 A1
Recreation Rd RDGW RG30 .... 39 H2
   WAR/TWY RG10 .... 27 H2
Rectory Cl EWKG RG40 .... 64 D1
Rectory Rd CAV/SC RG4 .... 33 H5
   EWKG RG40 .... 64 D2
Redberry Cl CAV/SC RG4 .... 34 C2
Red Cottage Dr CALC RG31 .... 47 F1 🔲
Red Cross Rd GOR/PANG RG8 .... 8 B3 🔲
Redgauntlet EWKG RG40 .... 69 H5 🔲
Redhatch Dr EARL RG6 .... 51 E3
Red Hl HEN RG9 .... 15 E4
Red House Cl EARL RG6 .... 51 C5
Red House Dr CAV/SC RG4 .... 13 C4
Redlake La EWKG RG40 .... 65 G5 🔲
Redlands Pl WWKG RG41 .... 70 A1
Redlands Rd READ RG1 .... 42 C5 🔲
Redruth Gdns WHIT RG2 .... 50 A4
Redwood Av WODY RG5 .... 44 D5
Redwood Wy CALC RG31 .... 31 G4
Reeds Av EARL RG6 .... 51 E2
Reeves Wy WWKG RG41 .... 64 B4
Regent Cl EARL RG6 .... 51 H4
Regent Ct READ RG1 .... 2 D3
Regent St READ RG1 .... 42 D3
Regis Cl WHIT RG2 .... 60 C1
Rembrandt Cl WWKG RG41 .... 63 G2 🔲
Rembrandt Wy READ RG1 .... 41 F5
Remenham Church La HEN RG9 .. 6 D2
Remenham La HEN RG9 .... 6 C4
Renault Rd WODY RG5 .... 44 D4
Repton Rd EARL RG6 .... 51 H2
Restwold Cl RDGW RG30 .... 48 D1 🔲
Retford Cl WODY RG5 .... 44 C1
Reynards Cl WWKG RG41 .... 53 F3
Rhigos CAV/SC RG4 .... 33 G1
Rhine Cl CAV/SC RG4 .... 34 C5
Rhodes Cl EARL RG6 .... 52 B2
Ribbleton Cl EARL RG6 .... 52 B2 🔲
Richborough Cl EARL RG6 .... 51 G3 🔲
Richfield Av READ RG1 .... 2 A1
Richfield Pl READ RG1 .... 2 B1
Richmond Ri WWKG RG41 .... 63 H1 🔲
Richmond Rd CAV/SC RG4 .... 33 F3
   RDGW RG30 .... 40 D2
Rickman Cl WHIT RG2 .... 68 B2
   WODY RG5 .... 44 A5
Rider's La THLE RG7 .... 58 B4
Ridge Hall Cl CAV/SC RG4 .... 33 F4
Ridgemount Cl CALC RG31 .... 31 E5 🔲
Ridgeway GOR/PANG RG8 .... 8 B1
Ridge Wy WAR/TWY RG10 .... 27 C2
The Ridgeway CAV/SC RG4 .... 33 H4
   WODY RG5 .... 44 C5
The Ridings CAV/SC RG4 .... 24 B4
Riding Wy WWKG RG41 .... 63 G2 🔲
Ridlington Cl EARL RG6 .... 52 B2
Righton Cl WAR/TWY RG10 .... 37 E4 🔲
Riley Rd RDGW RG30 .... 40 A2
Ringwood Rd RDGW RG30 .... 40 A1
Ripley Rd RDGW RG30 .... 40 B1
The Rise CAV/SC RG4 .... 34 A3
   WWKG RG41 .... 64 B1
Rissington Cl CALC RG31 .... 31 H4
Rivacres GOR/PANG RG8 .... 20 B1
Riverdene Dr WWKG RG41 .... 52 C2
River Gdns GOR/PANG RG8 .... 31 G2
Rivermead Rd WODY RG5 .... 44 C5
River Rd CAV/SC RG4 .... 33 E4
   READ RG1 .... 41 H4 🔲
Riversdale Ct READ RG1 .... 42 D2 🔲
Riverview Rd GOR/PANG RG8 ...... 29 H1
Roberts Gv WWKG RG41 .... 64 A5
Robin Cl THLE RG7 .... 57 E5 🔲
Robindale Av EARL RG6 .... 52 A2
Robinhood La WWKG RG41 .... 53 F3
Robin Hood Wy WWKG RG41 ...... 53 F2

Robinson Ct EARL RG6 51
Robin Wy CALC RG31 39
Rochester Av WODY RG5 44
Rockbourne Gdns RDGW RG30 .. 40
Rodway Rd RDGW RG30 39
Roebuck Ri CALC RG31 31
Rokeby Dr CAV/SC RG4 23
Roman Wy EARL RG6 52
Romany Cl RDGW RG30 40
Romany La RDGW RG30 40
Romsey Rd RDGW RG30 40
Rona Ct RDGW RG30 40
Rook Cl WWKG RG41 63
Rosebay EWKG RG40 55
Rosebery Rd CAV/SC RG4 23
Rose Cl WODY RG5 45
Rosecroft Wy WHIT RG2 60
Rosedale Crs EARL RG6 43
Rosehill Pk CAV/SC RG4 24
Rose Kiln La WHIT RG2 60
Rosemary Av EARL RG6 51
Rosemead Av CALC RG31 31
Rose St EWKG RG40 64
Rose Wk READ RG1 2
Rosewood WODY RG5 44
Roslyn Rd WODY RG5 40
Rossendale Rd CAV/SC RG4 34
Rossington Pl WHIT RG2 50
Ross Rd READ RG1 2
Rotherfield Av WWKG RG41 64
Rotherfield Cl THLE RG7 46
Rotherfield Rd HEN RG9 16
Rotherfield Wy CAV/SC RG4 33
Rothwell Gdns WODY RG5 44
Roundabouts La WWKG RG41 53
Roundhead Rd THLE RG7 46
Routh La RDGW RG30 39
Rowallan Cl CAV/SC RG4 34
Rowan Cl CAV/SC RG4 13
   WWKG RG41 64
Rowan Dr WODY RG5 44
Rowan Wy RDGW RG30 57
Rowcroft Rd WHIT RG2 68
Rowdell Dr WHIT RG2 50
Rowe Ct RDGW RG30 40
Rowland Wy EARL RG6 51
Row La CAV/SC RG4 24
Rowley Rd WHIT RG2 50
Royal Av CALC RG31 47
Royal Wy WHIT RG2 6
Roycroft La EWKG RG40 69
Royston Cl RDGW RG30 40
Ruby Cl WWKG RG41 .... 63 🔲
Rufus Isaacs Rd CAV/SC RG4 34
Rupert Cl HEN RG9 6
Rupert St READ RG1 42
Ruscombe La WAR/TWY RG10 37
Ruscombe Pk WAR/TWY RG10.... 37
Rushall Cl EARL RG6 60
Rushbrook Rd WODY RG5 44
Rushden Dr WHIT RG2 50
Rushey Wy EARL RG6 51
Rushmoor Gdns CALC RG31 47
Ruskin Wy WWKG RG41 63
Russell Rd CAV/SC RG4 23
Russell St READ RG1 2
Russell Wy WWKG RG41 53
Russet Cl CAV/SC RG4 13
Russet Gld CAV/SC RG4 24
Russley Gn EWKG RG40 70
Rustington Cl EARL RG6 51
Rutland Rd RDGW RG30 41
Rydal Av RDGW RG30 32
Ryecroft Cl WAR/TWY RG10 27
   WODY RG5 44
Ryeish La THLE RG7 60
Ryhill Wy EARL RG6 50
Rylstone Rd RDGW RG30 41

S

Sackville St READ RG1 2
Sadler's Ct WWKG RG41 53
Sadlers End WWKG RG41 63
Sadler's La WWKG RG41 53
The Sadlers CALC RG31 39
Saffron Cl EARL RG6 51
Sage Cl EARL RG6 51
Sage Rd CALC RG31 31
St Andrews Cl CWTH RG45 71
St Andrew's Rd CAV/SC RG4 33
   HEN RG9 16
St Anne's Cl HEN RG9 6
St Anne's Rd CAV/SC RG4 33
St Barnabas Rd CAV/SC RG4 33
   WHIT RG2 60

artholomews Rd *EARL* RG6...... **43** E3
irinus Rd *CALC* RG31 .... **39** F5 🔲
atherine's Cl *WWKG* RG41 ...... **52** D4
lements Cl *EARL* RG6 .... **51** H4 🔲
avid's Cl *CAV/SC* RG4 .... **33** G2
dward's Rd *EARL* RG6.............. **43** F4
lizabeth Cl *WHIT* RG2 .... **60** A1 🔲
iles Rd *EARL* RG1 .... **3** F7
iles Ct *READ* RG1 .... **3** F7
ves Cl *EWKG* RG41 .... **64** C5
ames Cl *GOR/PANG* RG8 .... **29** H1
AR/TWY* RG10 .... **37** H2
ames Rd *EWKG* RG40.............. **69** H3
ohns Cl *WODY* RG5................ **44** C2
ohn's Hl *READ* RG1................ **3** J5
ohn's Rd *CAV/SC* RG4 .... **34** B5
EAD* RG1 .... **3** J6
ohn's St *READ* RG1................ **3** J5
atherine's Rd *HEN* RG9 .... **16** A2
ukes Wy *CAV/SC* RG4.............. **34** A3
Mark's Rd *HEN* RG9................ **16** A1
Mary's Av *GOR/PANG* RG8 ...... **31** F2
Mary's Butts *READ* RG1 .... **2** E5
Mary's Cl *HEN* RG9................ **15** F1
Mary's Rd *WWKG* RG41 .... **53** E4
Mary's Wy *THLE* RG7 .... **57** F5 🔲
Michaels Cl *WAR/TWY* RG10 .... **37** H1
Michaels La *THLE* RG7 .... **56** A3
Michael's Rd *RDGW* RG30 ...... **39** H3 🔲
Patrick's Av *WAR/TWY* RG10 .... **36** D2
Paul's Ga *WWKG* RG41............ **64** B2
Peter's Av *CAV/SC* RG4 .... **33** F3
Peter's Hl *CAV/SC* RG4 .... **33** G4
Peter's Rd *EARL* RG6.............. **43** F4
Ronans Rd *RDGW* RG30 .... **40** C2
Saviour's Rd *READ* RG1 .... **41** G5
Sebastian's Cl *EWKG* RG40...... **71** F3
Stephens Cl *READ* RG1 .... **33** H5
combe Dr *EARL* RG6 .... **51** G1
combe Rd *WHIT* RG2 .... **50** C2
eby Cl *EARL* RG6 .... **52** B3
ford Cl *WHIT* RG2.................. **60** B1
isbury Cl *EARL* RG6 .... **70** B1
isbury Rd *RDGW* RG30 .... **41** F2
mon Cl *THLE* RG7.................. **66** A1
mond Rd *WHIT* RG2 .... **60** B2
tersgate Cl *EARL* RG6 .... **52** A3 🔲
mpage Cl *WHIT* RG2.............. **60** B2
nctuary Cl *RDGW* RG30 .... **39** H2
ndcroft Rd *EARL* RG6 .... **33** F1
ndford Cl *GOR/PANG* RG8 ...... **10** C1 🔲
ndford Dr *WODY* RG5 .... **44** C1
ndford La *WODY* RG5 .... **45** E3
ndgate Av *RDGW* RG30 .... **32** A5 🔲
ndhurst Rd *EWKG* RG40 .... **70** C3
ndleford Cl *WHIT* RG2 .... **60** B2 🔲
ndown Av *CALC* RG31 .... **47** E1
ndpit La *CAV/SC* RG4 .... **24** D3
ndringham Wy *CALC* RG31 ...... **47** E1 🔲
ndstone Cl *WWKG* RG41 .... **53** F4
ndy La *WWKG* RG41 .... **63** G4
ophire Cl *WWKG* RG41 .... **63** G1
rum Crs *EWKG* RG40 .... **65** E1
turn Cl *WWKG* RG41 .... **63** H2 🔲🔲
vernake Cl *RDGW* RG30 .... **40** A3 🔲
wpit Rd *WAR/TWY* RG10 .... **45** H3
wtry Cl *EARL* RG6 .... **52** B3 🔲
afell Cl *CALC* RG31 .... **47** H1 🔲
holars Cl *CAV/SC* RG4 .... **33** G4 🔲
hool Hl *WAR/TWY* RG10 .... **27** G3
hool La *CAV/SC* RG4 .... **34** A2
READ RG1 .... **33** H5
WAR/TWY RG10 .... **27** G2
hool Rd *CALC* RG31 .... **39** G2
EWKG RG40 .... **65** E2 🔲
RDGW RG30 .... **57** F2
WHIT RG2 .... **68** C1
hool Ter *READ* RG1................ **42** C2
ots Dr *WWKG* RG41 .... **53** H5
ott Cl *CAV/SC* RG4 .... **33** H2
WODY RG5 .... **44** D3
ours La *RDGW* RG30 .... **40** C1
aford Gdns *WODY* RG5 .... **44** B4
aford Rd *EWKG* RG40 .... **65** E2
arles Farm La *RDGW* RG30 .... **48** C4
aton Gdns *WHIT* RG2 .... **50** B3
dgefield Cl *EARL* RG6 .... **13** G3
dgewell Rd *CAV/SC* RG4 .... **13** G4
lborne Gdns *RDGW* RG30 ...... **40** B1
lcourt Cl *WODY* RG5.............. **44** D3
llafield Wy *EARL* RG6 .... **51** H3
lsdon Av *WODY* RG5 .... **44** C2
lsey Wy *EARL* RG6 .... **51** G5
lva Ct *READ* RG1 .... **42** B4
nd Rd *CAV/SC* RG4 .... **3** J1

Seton Dr *CALC* RG31 .... **40** A5 🔲
Sevenoaks Dr *THLE* RG7 .... **59** H5
Sevenoaks Rd *EARL* RG6 .... **51** G2
Severn Wy *RDGW* RG30............ **40** A4
Sewell Cl *CAV/SC* RG4 .... **33** G2
Seymour Av *WHIT* RG2 .... **60** D3
Shackleton Wy *WODY* RG5........ **44** D3
Shaftesbury Rd *RDGW* RG30 .... **40** C2
Shakespeare Cl *CAV/SC* RG4 .... **34** C2 🔲
Sharnwood Dr *CALC* RG31 ...... **40** A5
Sharpethorpe Cl *EARL* RG6 ...... **51** G4 🔲
Shaw Rd *READ* RG1 .... **41** G4
Sheep Wk *CAV/SC* RG4 .... **34** A3
Sheepways La *CAV/SC* RG4........ **22** C4
Sheerlands Rd *EWKG* RG40 ...... **68** B5
Shefford Crs *EWKG* RG40 .... **55** E5
Shelley Cl *WODY* RG5 .... **52** B1 🔲
Shenstone Cl *EWKG* RG40 .... **70** B3 🔲
Shenstone Rd *WHIT* RG2 .... **50** A1
Shepherds Av *EARL* RG6 .... **43** G2
Shepherds Hl *EARL* RG6 .... **43** H2 🔲
Shepherd's House La
EARL RG6 .... **43** F2 🔲
Shepley Dr *CAV/SC* RG4 .... **33** F4
Shepley Dr *RDGW* RG30.......... **48** D1
Sheraton Dr *CALC* RG31.......... **39** E1
Sherbourne Dr *WODY* RG5 ...... **44** C2
Sherfield Cl *WHIT* RG2 .... **50** C1
Sherfield Dr *WHIT* RG2 .... **50** C1
Sheridan Av *CAV/SC* RG4 .... **33** G3
Sheridan Wy *WWKG* RG41........ **63** H3
Sherman Rd *READ* RG1 .... **3** F7
READ RG1 .... **42** A4
Sherwood Gdns *HEN* RG9 .... **15** H1
Sherwood Ri *GOR/PANG* RG8.... **31** E3
Sherwood Rd *WWKG* RG41 ...... **53** F3
Sherwood Rd *RDGW* RG30........ **40** D2
Shilling Cl *RDGW* RG30 .... **40** C4 🔲
Shinfield Ri *WHIT* RG2 .... **50** D1
Shinfield Rd *WHIT* RG2 .... **50** D4
Shiplake Bottom *HEN* RG9 ...... **13** F2
Shipley Cl *WODY* RG5.............. **44** B1
Shipton Cl *CALC* RG31 .... **31** F5
Shire's Head Cl *RDGW* RG30 .... **41** E4 🔲
The Shires *WWKG* RG41............ **64** B1
Shirley Av *WHIT* RG2 .... **60** B1
Shirvell's Hl *GOR/PANG* RG8 .... **10** A2
Shooter's Hl *GOR/PANG* RG8 .... **19** E4
Shooters Wy *WHIT* RG2 .... **49** G5
Shortheath La *THLE* RG7.......... **56** A5
Short St *CAV/SC* RG4 .... **34** A5
GOR/PANG RG8 .... **30** A2 🔲
READ RG1 .... **42** A4
The Short *GOR/PANG* RG8........ **31** G2
Shrubland Dr *RDGW* RG30........ **48** B1
Shute End *EWKG* RG40 .... **56** A2
Sibley Park Rd *EARL* RG6 .... **51** F4
Sibson *EARL* RG6 .... **51** F4
Sidmouth Grange Cl *EARL* RG6 .. **43** G3
Sidmouth Grange Rd *EARL* RG6 .. **43** G3
Sidmouth St *READ* RG1 .... **3** H5
Silbury Cl *CALC* RG31 .... **47** E1 🔲
Silchester Rd *RDGW* RG30........ **48** D1
Silver Birches *WWKG* RG41 ...... **63** F5 🔲
Silverdale Rd *EARL* RG6 .... **51** G2
WAR/TWY RG10 .... **27** C3
Silver Fox Crs *WODY* RG5 .... **44** A4
Silver St *READ* RG1 .... **3** G7
Silverthorne Dr *CAV/SC* RG4...... **33** E1
Simmonds St *READ* RG1 .... **2** E6
Simmons Flds *WAR/TWY* RG10 .. **37** E4
Simmons Rd *HEN* RG9 .... **6** A3
Simon's Cl *WWKG* RG41 .... **31** F3 🔲
Simon's La *WWKG* RG41 .... **53** G5
Sindle Cl *WWKG* RG41 .... **53** G5
Sindlesham Rd *WHIT* RG2 .... **62** B5
Singers Cl *HEN* RG9 .... **16** B1
Sirius Cl *WWKG* RG41 .... **64** A2 🔲
Skarries Vw *CAV/SC* RG4 .... **23** E4
Skeffling Cl *EARL* RG6 .... **52** B3 🔲
Skelmerdale Wy *EARL* RG6 ...... **52** B2
Skerritt Wy *GOR/PANG* RG8 .... **31** G3
Skilton Rd *CALC* RG31 .... **31** F4
Skye Cl *CALC* RG31 .... **47** H1 🔲
The Slopes *CAV/SC* RG4 .... **34** C5
Smallmead Rd *WHIT* RG2 .... **13** G4
Smith Cl *CAV/SC* RG4 .... **13** G4
Snowberry Cl *WWKG* RG41 ...... **64** A3
Snowden Dr *CALC* RG31 .... **38** D4 🔲
Snowdrop Gv *WWKG* RG41 ...... **53** F2
Soane End *CAV/SC* RG4 .... **33** H1
Soham Cl *EARL* RG6 .... **51** H5 🔲🔲
Soldiers Ri *EWKG* RG40 .... **71** E4
Somerset Cl *WWKG* RG41 .... **63** G2 🔲
Somerstown Ct *READ* RG1........ **2** B6
Somerton Gdns *EARL* RG6 ...... **51** F3
Somerville Cl *WWKG* RG41 ...... **63** G4 🔲
Sonning La *CAV/SC* RG4 .... **36** A5

Sonning Mdw *CAV/SC* RG4 ...... **43** H1
Sopwith Cl *WODY* RG5............ **44** D3 🔲
Sorrel Cl *EWKG* RG40 .... **55** F5
THLE RG7 .... **57** E5 🔲
Southampton St *READ* RG1 ...... **3** F7
South Av *HEN* RG9 .... **16** B1
South Cl *EWKG* RG40 .... **64** D3
Southcote Farm La *RDGW* RG50 .. **41** E5
Southcote La *RDGW* RG30 .... **41** E5
Southcote Rd *RDGW* RG30 ...... **41** E4
Southdown Rd *CAV/SC* RG4 ...... **34** A2
South Dr *CAV/SC* RG4 .... **43** H1
EARL RG6 .... **51** E3
EWKG RG40 .... **64** D3
THLE RG7 .... **57** E5
Southerndene Cl *CALC* RG31 .... **31** G5 🔲
Southern Hl *READ* RG1 .... **42** D5
Southglade *WHIT* RG2 .... **50** C5 🔲
South Lake Crs *WODY* RG5 ...... **44** B5
Southlands Cl *EWKG* RG40 ...... **65** E3
Southlands Rd *EWKG* RG40 ...... **65** E4
South St *READ* RG1 .... **3** G6
READ RG1 .... **34** A5
South View Av *CAV/SC* RG4...... **34** A5
Southview Cl *WAR/TWY* RG10 .. **37** H1 🔲
South View Pk *CAV/SC* RG4 ...... **34** B5
Southwold Cl *EARL* RG6 .... **52** A3
Southwood *EWKG* RG40 .... **65** E4
Southwood Gdns *THLE* RG7 ...... **56** D5
Sovereign Wy *CALC* RG31 .... **39** F5 🔲
Span Hl *HEN* RG9 .... **25** G5
Sparrow Cl *WWKG* RG41 .... **63** H3 🔲
Spencer Cl *WWKG* RG41 .... **63** G2 🔲
Spencer Rd *WHIT* RG2 .... **60** A1
Spey Rd *RDGW* RG30 .... **40** B2
Spinney Cl *CAV/SC* RG4 .... **24** A5 🔲
The Spinney *EWKG* RG40.......... **70** A3
Spitfire Wy *WODY* RG5 .... **44** D3
Spode Cl *RDGW* RG30 .... **39** H2
Spring Cl *GOR/PANG* RG8 .... **28** C2
Springdale *EARL* RG6 .... **51** G3
EWKG RG40 .... **69** H3
Springfield End *GOR/PANG* RG8 .. **8** B1 🔲
Springfield Pk *WAR/TWY* RG10 .. **37** H3
Spring Gdns *THLE* RG7 .... **66** A2
Spring Gv *READ* RG1 .... **42** B4
Springhill Rd *GOR/PANG* RG8 .. **8** B1
Spring La *CAV/SC* RG4 .... **35** C1
Spring Wk *WAR/TWY* RG10 ...... **27** G3 🔲
Springwood La *HEN* RG9 .... **13** C1
Spruce Rd *WODY* RG5 .... **44** D4
The Spur *WAR/TWY* RG10 .... **27** H1 🔲
The Square *THLE* RG7 .... **66** A1
Squirrels Wy *EARL* RG6 .... **51** G3
Stable Cl *THLE* RG7 .... **56** D5
Staddlestone Cl *CALC* RG31 .... **31** F5 🔲
Stadium Wy *RDGW* RG30 .... **40** C1
Stafford Cl *WODY* RG5 .... **44** C3
Staffordshire Cl *RDGW* RG30 .. **40** A1 🔲
Stanham Rd *RDGW* RG30 .... **40** A2 🔲
Stanhope Rd *WHIT* RG2 .... **50** C2
Stanley Gv *READ* RG1 .... **2** A4
Stanley Rd *EWKG* RG40 .... **65** F2
Stanley St *READ* RG1 .... **2** B4
Stanshawe Rd *READ* RG1 .... **2** D3
Stanton Cl *EARL* RG6 .... **51** H1
Stapleford Rd *RDGW* RG30 ...... **48** D1 🔲
Starling Cl *WWKG* RG41 .... **64** A3
Starlings Dr *CALC* RG31 .... **39** E5
Starmead Dr *EWKG* RG40 .... **65** E3
Star Rd *CAV/SC* RG4 .... **34** B5
Station Ap *READ* RG1.............. **2** E3
Station Hl *READ* RG1 .... **2** E3
Station Rd *EARL* RG6 .... **51** H1
EWKG RG40 .... **64** C2
GOR/PANG RG8 .... **8** B3
HEN RG9 .... **6** B5
HEN RG9 .... **16** B5
READ RG1 .... **2** E4
THLE RG7 .... **46** B2
WAR/TWY RG10 .... **27** F3
WAR/TWY RG10 .... **37** G3
Staverton Cl *EWKG* RG40 .... **65** G2 🔲
Staverton Rd *WHIT* RG2 .... **50** B2
Steeple Wk *EARL* RG6 .... **51** E5
Steggles Cl *WODY* RG5 .... **44** A2
Stephanie Chase Ct
EWKG RG40 .... **65** E1 🔲
Stephenson Rd *WHIT* RG2 ...... **68** D4
Sterling Wy *RDGW* RG30.......... **40** B1
Stevens La *HEN* RG9 .... **13** E1
Stilton Cl *EARL* RG6 .... **52** B3 🔲🔲
Stirling Cl *CAV/SC* RG4 .... **34** C1
Stockbury Cl *EARL* RG6 .... **51** G4
Stockton Rd *WHIT* RG2 .... **50** B4
Stoke Row Rd *HEN* RG9 .... **13** F1
Stokes Vw *GOR/PANG* RG8 ...... **29** H2
Stonea Cl *EARL* RG6 .... **51** H5 🔲🔲

Stoneham Cl *RDGW* RG30........ **40** B4
Stonehaven Dr *WODY* RG5 ...... **44** D4
Stone St *RDGW* RG30 .... **40** C1
Stour Cl *RDGW* RG30 .... **40** B2 🔲
Stow Rd *HEN* RG9 .... **16** C1
St Patrick's Br *WAR/TWY* RG10 .. **36** C1
Strachey Cl *GOR/PANG* RG8...... **29** H4
Strand Wy *EARL* RG6 .... **51** G4
Stratford Wy *CALC* RG31.......... **38** C1
Stratheden Pl *READ* RG1.......... **2** C4
Strathmore Dr *WAR/TWY* RG10 .. **36** D3
Strathy Cl *RDGW* RG30 .... **40** C2
Stratton Gdns *WHIT* RG2........ **50** B4
The Street *THLE* RG7 .... **66** B5
Stuart Cl *CAV/SC* RG4 .... **34** A2
Studland Cl *WHIT* RG2 .... **60** B1 🔲
Sturbridge Cl *EARL* RG6 .... **51** H4 🔲
Sturges Rd *EWKG* RG40 .... **64** D3
Suffolk Cl *WWKG* RG41 .... **63** G2 🔲
Suffolk Rd *RDGW* RG30 .... **40** D3 🔲
Sulham La *GOR/PANG* RG8 ...... **30** B3
Sulhamstead Rd *THLE* RG7........ **56** C4
Summerfield Cl *WWKG* RG41 .. **54** A4
Summerfield Ri *GOR/PANG* RG8 .. **8** C2
Summit Cl *EWKG* RG40 .... **70** A5
Sunderland Cl *WODY* RG5 ...... **45** E2
Sundew Cl *EWKG* RG40 .... **65** F1
Sundial Cl *RDGW* RG30 .... **40** B4 🔲
Sun St *READ* RG1 .... **42** C3
Surley Rw *CAV/SC* RG4 .... **33** H2
Sussex Gdns *WODY* RG5 .... **44** B3
Sussex La *THLE* RG7 .... **66** B2
Sutcliffe Av *EARL* RG6 .... **52** A2
Sutherland Gv *CALC* RG31 ...... **47** H1
Sutherlands Av *READ* RG1 ...... **42** B5
Suttons Park Av *EARL* RG6 ...... **43** E2
READ RG1 .... **42** D2
Swainstone Rd *WHIT* RG2 ...... **42** A5
Swallow Cl *CALC* RG31 .... **39** F4 🔲
Swallowfield Dr *WHIT* RG2 ...... **60** B4
Swallow Field Gdns *THLE* RG7 .. **46** B1 🔲
Swallowfield Rd *THLE* RG7........ **67** F4
Swallow Wy *WWKG* RG41 .... **63** H3
Swanmore Cl *EARL* RG6 .... **52** B4
Swan Pl *READ* RG1 .... **2** E6
Swanscourt *WAR/TWY* RG10 .... **37** H4 🔲
Swansea Rd *READ* RG1 .... **2** D2
Swansea Ter *CALC* RG31 .... **39** C1
Swanston Fld *GOR/PANG* RG8 .. **20** A5
Sweetbriar *CWTH* RG45 .... **71** H4 🔲
Sweet Briar Dr *CALC* RG31 ...... **47** F1 🔲🔲
Swepstone Cl *EARL* RG6 .... **51** H3
Swift Cl *WWKG* RG41 .... **63** H5 🔲
Swinbrook Cl *CALC* RG31 .... **31** G4
Swiss Cottage Cl *CALC* RG31 .. **39** F2 🔲
Sycamore Cl *RDGW* RG30 .... **57** E3
WODY RG5 .... **43** H5
Sycamore Dr *WAR/TWY* RG10 .. **37** G2
Sycamore Rd *WHIT* RG2 .... **50** D3
Sylvester Cl *WAR/TWY* RG10 .... **53** G2

T

Taff Cl *RDGW* RG30 .... **40** B3
Talbot Cl *CAV/SC* RG4 .... **34** C5
Talbot Ct *READ* RG1 .... **2** D6
Talbot Wy *CALC* RG31 .... **31** F4 🔲
Talfourd Av *EARL* RG6 .... **43** F5
Tallis La *RDGW* RG30 .... **49** E1
Tamar Gdns *WHIT* RG2 .... **50** B2
Tamarind Wy *EARL* RG6 .... **51** E4
Tamarisk Av *WHIT* RG2 .... **50** D4
Tamarisk Ri *EWKG* RG40 .... **64** D1
Tamar Wy *WWKG* RG41 .... **63** H2
Tamworth Cl *EARL* RG6 .... **51** H4 🔲
Tanglewood *EWKG* RG40 .... **70** B4
Tangley Dr *WWKG* RG41 .... **64** C4
Tanhouse La *WWKG* RG41 ...... **64** B3
Tanners La *CAV/SC* RG4 .... **23** G4
Targett Ct *WWKG* RG41 .... **53** E3 🔲
Tarlton Ct *RDGW* RG30 .... **39** H4
Tarragon Cl *EARL* RG6 .... **51** E4 🔲
Tarragon Wy *THLE* RG7 .... **57** E5
Tattersall Cl *EWKG* RG40 .... **65** F3
Tavistock Rd *WHIT* RG2 .... **50** A2
Tay Rd *RDGW* RG30 .... **40** B2
Tazewell Ct *READ* RG1 .... **2** A7
Telford Crs *WODY* RG5 .... **44** C1
Temple Ms *WODY* RG5 .... **44** C3
Temple Pl *READ* RG1 .... **2** E7
Templeton Gdns *WHIT* RG2 .... **50** B4 🔲
Tenby Av *CAV/SC* RG4 .... **34** C2
Tennyson Rd *WODY* RG5 .... **52** B1
Tern Cl *RDGW* RG30 .... **40** B4
The Terrace *EWKG* RG40 .... **64** C2 🔲
Tessa Rd *READ* RG1 .... **2** B1

...dermere Cl *WWKG* RG41 ...... 53 F2 🔲
...dermere Rd *WHIT* RG2 .... 50 C2
...dmill Av *WWKG* RG41 .... 53 H5
...drush Wy *RDGW* RG30 .... 40 C3 🔲
...dsor Ride *EWKG* RG40 .... 70 B4
...dsor Wy *CALC* RG31 .... 47 E1 🔢
...gate Rd *WODY* RG5 .... 44 B4
...grove Rd *RDGW* RG30 .... 40 D4
...kfield Cl *WHIT* RG2 .... 64 C5
...nersh Ga *WWKG* RG41 .... 53 G3
...nersh Gv *WWKG* RG41 .... 53 F4
...ser Dr *RDGW* RG30 .... 49 E1
...ston Cl *THLE* RG7 .... 66 C1
...terberry Wy *CAV/SC* RG4 ..... 33 F3
...ton Rd *WHIT* RG2 .... 50 C5
...tringham Wy
...*OR/PANG* RG8 .... 31 G2
...e's Firs *THLE* RG7 .... 56 A5
...pington Cl *EARL* RG6 .... 52 A3
...teria Cl *WWKG* RG41 ..... 64 A3 🔟
...ton Ter *READ* RG1 .... 3 F4
...cham Cl *EARL* RG6 .... 52 A5 🔲
...tenham Av *CALC* RG31 .... 39 E2
...tenham Cl
...*OR/PANG* RG8 .... 10 C1 🔢
...burn Cl *CAV/SC* RG4 .... 33 F3
...kingham Rd *EARL* RG6 .... 42 D3
...lseley St *READ* RG1.......... 2 D7
...odbine Cl *EARL* RG6 .... 51 H4 🔲

Woodbridge Rd *CALC* RG31 .... 39 E4 🔲
Woodcock Ct *THLE* RG7 .... 59 H4
Woodcote Rd *CAV/SC* RG4 ...... 33 F3
Woodcote St *CAV/SC* RG4 ...... 33 E2
Woodfield Wy *THLE* RG7 .... 46 B1 🔲
Woodford Cl *CAV/SC* RG4 .... 33 F3
Wood Gn *GOR/PANG* RG8 .... 10 B1 🔲
Wood Green Cl *RDGW* RG30 ..... 41 F3
Woodhurst La *WWKG* RG41 ..... 54 A4 🔲
Woodland Av *WWKG* RG41 ...... 53 H5
Woodland Dr *RDGW* RG30 ...... 39 G3
Woodlands Av *THLE* RG7 .... 56 D5
   WODY RG5 .... 44 A3
Woodlands Gv *CAV/SC* RG4 ..... 34 C3
Woodlands Rd *CAV/SC* RG4 ..... 13 F3
   HEN RG9 .... 16 B5
The Woodlands *WWKG* RG41 .... 63 G4
Wood La *CAV/SC* RG4 .... 12 C5
   CAV/SC RG4 .... 13 C4
   GOR/PANG RG8 .... 10 A1
   WHIT RG2 .... 68 C1
Woodley Gn *WODY* RG5 .... 44 C2
Woodman Cl *WHIT* RG2 .... 60 B2 🔲
Woodman's La *THLE* RG7 .... 56 C5
Woodpecker Cl *WAR/TWY* RG10 .. 37 H4
Woodrow Dr *EWKG* RG40 .... 65 F2
Woodsend *EARL* RG6 .... 50 D5
Woodside Cl *EWKG* RG40 .... 69 H3 🔲

Woodside La *CAV/SC* RG4 .... 12 D4
Woodside Wy *WHIT* RG2 .... 60 C1
Woods Rd *CAV/SC* RG4 .... 34 C3
Woodstock St *READ* RG1 .... 42 C3
Woodview Rd *GOR/PANG* RG8 ... 30 A2 🔲
Woodward Cl *WWKG* RG41 ...... 53 G3
Woodwaye *WODY* RG5 .... 44 A3
Woodyer Cl *WODY* RG5 .... 44 B5
Woolacombe Dr *EARL* RG6 ...... 50 D3
Woosehill *WWKG* RG41 .... 63 H2
Woosehill La *WWKG* RG41....... 64 A2
Wootton Cl *CALC* RG31 .... 39 F2 🔲
Wootton Rd *HEN* RG9 .... 15 H1
Worcester Cl *RDGW* RG30 ...... 40 B5
Worrall Wy *EARL* RG6 .... 51 E5
Worsley Pl *THLE* RG7 .... 46 B2
Worton Dr *WHIT* RG2........... 49 H5
Wren Cl *THLE* RG7 .... 57 E5 🔲
   WWKG RG41 .... 63 H3
Wrenfield Dr *CAV/SC* RG4 .... 33 G2
Wrenswood Cl *WHIT* RG2 .... 60 A2
Wroxham Rd *WODY* RG5 .... 44 A2
Wychcotes *READ* RG1........... 33 G5
Wychelm Rd *WHIT* RG2 .... 60 D3
Wychwood Cl *EARL* RG6 .... 51 E3
Wychwood Crs *EARL* RG6 .... 51 E2
Wye Cl *RDGW* RG30 .... 40 A4
Wyfold La *CAV/SC* RG4 .... 12 B2
   HEN RG9 .... 13 F1
Wykeham Rd *EARL* RG6 .... 43 F1

Wyncote Cl *WHIT* RG2 .... 51 E4
Wyndale Cl *HEN* RG9 .... 6 B5
Wyndham Crs *WODY* RG5........ 44 A1
Wynford Cl *RDGW* RG30 .... 48 D1 🔲
Wyre Ct *CALC* RG31 .... 31 F4

Y

Yarnold Cl *EWKG* RG40 .... 65 G1 🔲
Yarnton Cl *CAV/SC* RG4 .... 34 B1
Yelverton Rd *WHIT* RG2 .... 50 B2
Yew Cl *WWKG* RG41 .... 64 A3
Yewhurst Cl *WAR/TWY* RG10 .... 37 F1
Yew La *READ* RG1.............. 49 G1
Yew Tree Ct *GOR/PANG* RG8 .... 8 B3 🔲
Yew Tree Ri *CALC* RG31 .... 39 F5
Yield Hall La *READ* RG1 .... 3 F5
Yield Hall Pl *READ* RG1 .... 3 F5
Yoreham Cl *EARL* RG6 .... 52 B4 🔲
York Rd *HEN* RG9 .... 6 A4
   READ RG1 .... 2 D2

Z

Zinnia Cl *WWKG* RG41 .... 63 G1 🔲
Zinzan St *READ* RG1 .... 2 C5

Index - featured places

...e Abbey School
   READ RG1 .... 42 B4
...e Business Park
   WHIT RG2 .... 50 A5
...lington School
   WODY RG5 .... 44 C4
...red Sutton Primary School
   EARL RG6 .... 43 E4
...Saints Infants School
   READ RG1 .... 2 A6
...bulance Station
   READ RG1 .... 2 C4
...orfield C of E School
   WHIT RG2 .... 62 C5
...ade Gallery
   GOR/PANG RG8 .... 8 A3
...e Argyle Clinic
   READ RG1 .... 2 A5
... Gallery
   HEN RG9 .... 6 B4
...e Art Gallery
   READ RG1 .... 2 E6
...hur Hill Memorial
...Swimming Baths
   READ RG1 .... 42 C3
...mead School
   WHIT RG2 .... 50 B4
...ction Market
   READ RG1 .... 2 C3
...e Avenue School
   WHIT RG2 .... 50 B1
...gdemore Cp School
   HEN RG9 .... 5 H4
...sildon House
   GOR/PANG RG8 .... 18 D3
...ttle Farm Trading Estate
   TLHT RG30 .... 41 E1
...ttle Primary School
   TLHT RG30 .... 40 D3
...arwood College
   WWKG RG41 .... 63 G1
...arwood Primary School
   WWKG RG41 .... 53 F4
...echwood County
...Junior & Infant School
   WODY RG5 .... 44 B3
...e Bell Surgery
   HEN RG9 .... 6 A4
...rkshire County Council
   READ RG1 .... 3 G5
...ch Copse Primary School
   CALC RG31 .... 39 F2
...akes Lock Museum
   READ RG1 .... 3 K4
...athouse Surgery
   GOR/PANG RG8 .... 8 A3
...hun Gallery
   HEN RG9 .... 6 B5
...ookfields School
   CALC RG31 .... 31 F4
...ookside Business Centre
   THLE RG7 .... 66 C5
...e Brookside Group Practice
   EARL RG6 .... 52 A2

Building Design School
   WHIT RG2 .... 61 E4
The Bulmershe School
   EARL RG6 .... 43 H3
Burghfield Aqua Sports Club
   TLHT RG30 .... 48 B4
Burghfield Health Centre
   THLE RG7 .... 57 E5
Burma Hills Surgery
   EWKG RG40 .... 65 E1
Bus Depot
   READ RG1 .... 2 C3
The Business Centre
   WWKG RG41 .... 64 C4
Calcot Junior and Infant School
   CALC RG31 .... 47 E1
Castle Hill Clinic
   READ RG1 .... 2 B6
Caversham Park Primary School
   CAV/SC RG4 .... 34 D1
Caversham Primary School
   CAV/SC RG4 .... 33 H4
Cedar Park School
   WAR/TWY RG10 .... 37 F2
Centenary Business Park
   HEN RG9 .... 6 C5
Central Swimming Pool
   READ RG1 .... 2 B4
Century Galleries
   HEN RG9 .... 6 B4
Chalfont Surgery
   EARL RG6 .... 51 F4
Chapel Hill Surgery
   CALC RG31 .... 39 F2
Chatham Street Surgery
   READ RG1 .... 2 C5
Chiltern Edge Secondary School
   CAV/SC RG4 .... 13 F5
Christchurch Primary School
   WHIT RG2 .... 42 A5
Christ the King School
   WHIT RG2 .... 50 B5
The Clinic
   READ RG1 .... 2 D5
Coley Park School
   READ RG1 .... 41 F5
Coley Park Surgery
   READ RG1 .... 41 F5
Coley Primary School
   READ RG1 .... 2 D7
Colleton Cp School
   WAR/TWY RG10 .... 37 H4
Coombe Infants School
   READ RG1 .... 62 B5
Crosfields School
   READ RG1 .... 50 D5
Curtain Gallery
   WWKG RG41 .... 53 F4
David Lloyd Sports Centre
   EARL RG6 .... 43 F1
Delwood Hospital
   TLHT RG30 .... 40 D4
Downs Way School
   CALC RG31 .... 31 F4

Dryleas Sports Ground
   HEN RG9 .... 6 A3
Duffield Road Cp School
   WODY RG5 .... 44 C1
Ebony Health Centre
   WAR/TWY RG10 .... 37 G2
Embbrook County
...Junior & Infant School
   WWKG RG41 .... 54 A4
The Embbrook School
   WWKG RG41 .... 54 A5
Emmer Green Clinic
   CAV/SC RG4 .... 34 A2
Emmer Green Cp School
   CAV/SC RG4 .... 34 A1
Emmer Green Surgery
   CAV/SC RG4 .... 33 H1
English Martyrs RC
...Primary School
   TLHT RG30 .... 40 B3
E P Collier School
   READ RG1 .... 2 D2
Fairview Trading Estate
   HEN RG9 .... 16 C1
Family Planning Clinic
   READ RG1 .... 3 J7
Fireplace Gallery
   EWKG RG40 .... 64 D2
Firestation
   READ RG1 .... 2 D2
Food Gallery
   READ RG1 .... 42 D2
Football Club
   HEN RG9 .... 16 C1
Forbury Retail Park
   READ RG1 .... 3 H4
The Forest
...Comprehensive School
   WWKG RG41 .... 53 E3
Friar's Walk Shopping Centre
   READ RG1 .... 2 E4
The Gallery
   CAV/SC RG4 .... 35 G2
Garlands County Junior School
   THLE RG7 .... 56 D5
George Palmer Junior School
   WHIT RG2 .... 50 B1
Gillotts School
   HEN RG9 .... 15 G2
Goring C of E Primary School
   GOR/PANG RG8 .... 8 B2
Gorse Ride Junior School
   EWKG RG40 .... 69 G4
Green Road Surgery
   EARL RG6 .... 43 E4
Gresham Way Industrial Estate
   TLHT RG30 .... 32 B3
Greys Gallery
   HEN RG9 .... 6 B5
Grovelands Surgery
   TLHT RG30 .... 40 C2
Gun Street Gallery
   READ RG1 .... 3 F5

The Hart Surgery
   HEN RG9 .... 6 A4
Hawkedon Primary School
   EARL RG6 .... 52 B3
Hawthorns Primary School
   WWKG RG41 .... 63 H1
The Health Centre
   WHIT RG2 .... 50 D2
Hemdean House School
   CAV/SC RG4 .... 33 H4
The Henley College
   .... 5 H5
Henley District Indoor
...Sports Centre
   HEN RG9 .... 15 G2
Henley Golf Club
   HEN RG9 .... 16 A3
Henley Town Football Club
   HEN RG9 .... 16 C1
Hernes Estate
   HEN RG9 .... 15 E1
The Hexagon
   READ RG1 .... 2 D5
Highdown School
   CAV/SC RG4 .... 33 H2
Highwood Primary School
   EARL RG6 .... 43 H4
The Hill Primary School
   CAV/SC RG4 .... 34 B2
Hillside Primary School
   EARL RG6 .... 51 E5
Hm Prison
   READ RG1 .... 3 H4
Holme Grange School
   EWKG RG40 .... 65 G5
The Holt School
   WWKG RG41 .... 64 C1
Ibis Sports Club
   CAV/SC RG4 .... 32 C5
The Junior School
   GOR/PANG RG8 .... 29 E2
Katesgrove Primary School
   READ RG1 .... 2 E7
Keep Hatch County
...Junior School
   EWKG RG40 .... 65 E1
Kendrick Girls School
   READ RG1 .... 3 G6
Kennet Surgery
   READ RG1 .... 42 D3
Kennet Valley Primary School
   TLHT RG30 .... 48 A1
Kenton Theatre
   HEN RG9 .... 6 B4
Kidmore End Primary School
   CAV/SC RG4 .... 23 E1
Langtree Secondary School
   GOR/PANG RG8 .... 10 C1
Leighton Park School
   WHIT RG2 .... 50 D2
Loddon County Infants School
   EARL RG6 .... 52 A2
Loddon County Junior School
   EARL RG6 .... 52 A2

The Loddon Vale Practice
WODY RG5 .... **44** D3
Loddon Valley Leisure Centre
EARL RG6 .... **51** F4
Long Barn Lane Surgery
WHIT RG2 .... **50** A2
Long Lane Primary School
GOR/PANG RG8 .... **31** E3
Luckley Oakfield School
WWKG RG41 .... **64** C5
Ludgrove Preparatory School
EWKG RG40 .... **65** E5
Maiden Erlegh School
EARL RG6 .... **51** G1
Manor County School
TLHT RG30 .... **48** B1
Mansbridge House School
EARL RG6 .... **43** E4
Mapledurhamhouse
CAV/SC RG4 .... **31** H1
Meadway
Comprehensive School
TLHT RG30 .... **40** A3
Meadway Sports Centre
TLHT RG30 .... **40** A4
Melrose Surgery
READ RG1 .... **3** J6
Micklands Cp School
CAV/SC RG4 .... **34** C3
The Micro Centre
WHIT RG2 .... **49** H2
The Mill at Sonning (theatre) Ltd
CAV/SC RG4 .... **35** H3
Milman Road Health Centre
WHIT RG2 .... **42** A5
Moorlands Primary School
TLHT RG30 .... **39** H3
Mulberry Business Park
WWKG RG41 .... **64** B4
The Museum of
Berkshire Aviation
WODY RG5 .... **45** E4
Newtown Junior & Infant School
READ RG1 .... **42** C2
Nimrod Industrial Estate
WHIT RG2 .... **41** H5
The Norton Practice
READ RG1 .... **3** H6
Oaklands Business Centre
WWKG RG41 .... **64** B5
Oaklands County Junior & Infant
School
CWTH RG45 .... **71** H5
Old Art Gallery
EWKG RG40 .... **71** F1
Oracle Shopping Centre
READ RG1 .... **3** F5
The Oratory Preparatory School
GOR/PANG RG8 .... **10** A5
The Oratory School
GOR/PANG RG8 .... **10** D1
Oxford Rd Surgery
READ RG1 .... **2** D5
Oxford Road Primary School
READ RG1 .... **2** A5
Paddock Road Industrial Estate
CAV/SC RG4 .... **3** K1
Palmer C of E Junior School
EWKG RG40 .... **65** E1
Pangbourne College
GOR/PANG RG8 .... **29** E4
Pangbourne Infants School
GOR/PANG RG8 .... **30** B2
Pangbourne Medical Centre
GOR/PANG RG8 .... **29** H1
Park Lane Primary School
CALC RG31 .... **39** F2
Parkside Business Park
WODY RG5 .... **44** B2
Peppard C of E School
HEN RG9 .... **13** H1
Phoenix Plaza Bowling Alley
EWKG RG40 .... **64** C3
Physiotherapy Surgery
GOR/PANG RG8 .... **30** A1
The Piggott C of E School
WAR/TWY RG10 .... **27** F4
P M S Health Centre
READ RG1 .... **42** B4
Polehampton County
Infant School
WAR/TWY RG10 .... **37** G2
Polehampton Junior School
WAR/TWY RG10 .... **37** G1
Presentation College
TLHT RG30 .... **41** E5
Princess Marina College
EWKG RG40 .... **68** C3
Progress Theatre
WHIT RG2 .... **42** B5

Prospect Foot Clinic
CAV/SC RG4 .... **33** H4
Prospect School
TLHT RG30 .... **40** B5
Purley C of E School
GOR/PANG RG8 .... **31** F2
Queen Annes School
CAV/SC RG4 .... **34** A4
Radstock Cp School
EARL RG6 .... **51** G3
Ranikhet Primary School
TLHT RG30 .... **40** B2
Reading Adult College
TLHT RG30 .... **40** D2
Reading Adult &
Community College
READ RG1 .... **33** H5
Reading Blue Coat School
CAV/SC RG4 .... **35** H4
Reading Borough Council
READ RG1 .... **2** D6
Reading Business Centre
READ RG1 .... **3** C6
Reading Clinic
READ RG1 .... **3** J6
Reading College of Technology
READ RG1 .... **43** E4
Reading County Court
READ RG1 .... **3** C4
Reading Girls School
WHIT RG2 .... **50** B2
Reading Leisure Centre
WHIT RG2 .... **50** B4
Reading Retail Park
TLHT RG30 .... **40** C1
Reading School
READ RG1 .... **3** K7
Reading Superbowl
CALC RG31 .... **46** D1
Reading University
READ RG1 .... **42** C5
Redlands Primary School
READ RG1 .... **42** D5
Register Office
READ RG1 .... **2** C7
Reme Museum
EWKG RG40 .... **68** D3
Retail Park
READ RG1 .... **3** J4
Rivermead Cp School
WODY RG5 .... **44** C4
Rivermead Leisure Centre
READ RG1 .... **33** G5
The River & Rowing
Museum at Henley
HEN RG9 .... **6** C5
Robert Cort Industrial Estate
WHIT RG2 .... **42** A5
Robert Piggott C of E
Infant School
WAR/TWY RG10 .... **27** H3
Robert Piggott C of E
Junior School
WAR/TWY RG10 .... **27** G3
Rosedale Clinic
READ RG1 .... **42** C5
Royal Berkshire &
Battle Hospital
TLHT RG30 .... **41** E2
Royal Berkshire Hospital
READ RG1 .... **3** J7
Rupert House School
HEN RG9 .... **6** B3
Russell Street Surgery
READ RG1 .... **2** C6
Ryeish Green
Comprehensive School
THLE RG7 .... **60** A4
Sacred Heart RC School
HEN RG9 .... **6** A5
St Annes RC Primary School
CAV/SC RG4 .... **34** A5
St Crispins Secondary School
EWKG RG40 .... **65** F2
St Crispins Sports Centre
EWKG RG40 .... **65** F2
St Dominic Savio RC (aided)
Primary School
WODY RG5 .... **44** A2
St Edwards School
TLHT RG30 .... **41** E3
St Johns C of E School
READ RG1 .... **3** J6
St Josephs Convent School
READ RG1 .... **42** D5
St Martins RC Primary School
CAV/SC RG4 .... **34** D1
St Marys All Saints C of E
Primary School
READ RG1 .... **41** F5

St Marys Preparatory School
HEN RG9 .... **16** B1
St Marys Primary School
TLHT RG30 .... **57** F2
St Michaels Primary School
TLHT RG30 .... **40** B4
St Pauls C of E Junior School
WWKG RG41 .... **64** B2
St Pauls RC Primary School
CALC RG31 .... **39** F3
St Peter C of E School
EARL RG6 .... **43** G5
St Sebastians Primary School
EWKG RG40 .... **71** F3
St Teresa RC Primary School
EWKG RG40 .... **65** E3
Sandmartins Golf Club
EWKG RG40 .... **70** C2
Shinfield C of E Junior School
WHIT RG2 .... **61** E4
Shinfield Infant School
WHIT RG2 .... **60** D4
Shiplake C of E Primary School
HEN RG9 .... **26** B2
Shiplake College
HEN RG9 .... **26** C3
Showcase Cinemas Reading
WODY RG5 .... **52** C1
Shute End Medical Practice
WWKG RG41 .... **64** C2
Sindlesham School
WWKG RG41 .... **62** C1
Sonning Church of
England Primary School
CAV/SC RG4 .... **36** A4
Sonning Common Cp School
CALC RG4 .... **13** G4
Sonning Common Health Centre
CAV/SC RG4 .... **13** G4
Southcote Clinic
TLHT RG30 .... **48** C1
Southcote Cp School
TLHT RG30 .... **48** D1
Southfields Special School
EWKG RG40 .... **65** E4
Southlake County Junior School
WODY RG5 .... **44** A5
Southlake Primary School
WODY RG5 .... **44** B5
21 South Street Arts Centrel
READ RG1 .... **3** C6
Springfield Primary School
CALC RG31 .... **39** E3
Stadium Industrial Estate
TLHT RG30 .... **40** C1
Station Industrial Estate
WWKG RG41 .... **64** C2
Superstore
READ RG1 .... **3** K3
Superstore
WHIT RG2 .... **50** A2
Suttons Business Park
READ RG1 .... **42** D2
Swallowfield Medical Practice
THLE RG7 .... **66** B4
Swallowfield Park
THLE RG7 .... **66** D3
Temple
READ RG1 .... **2** E6
The Temple
GOR/PANG RG8 .... **8** B1
Thames Gallery
HEN RG9 .... **6** B4
Thameside School
READ RG1 .... **34** A5
Thames Valley Business Park
EARL RG6 .... **43** G1
Theale C of E Primary School
THLE RG7 .... **46** A2
Theale Green School
THLE RG7 .... **46** A2
Theale Medical Centre
THLE RG7 .... **46** A2
Theatre & Arts Centre
WHIT RG2 .... **60** C1
Tilehurst Medical Centre
TLHT RG30 .... **39** H2
Tilehurst Parish Council
CALC RG31 .... **39** E5
Tilehurst Village Surgery
CALC RG31 .... **39** G2
Toutley Industrial Estate
WWKG RG41 .... **54** A3
Town Hall & Museum
READ RG1 .... **3** F4
Townlands Hospital
HEN RG9 .... **5** H4
Trinity Primary School
HEN RG9 .... **6** B5

Twyford Business Park
WAR/TWY RG10 .... **3**
Twyford Health Centre
WAR/TWY RG10 .... **3**
Unit 1 Laffords Industrial Estate
THLE RG7 .... **4**
University Health Centre
WHIT RG2 .... **5**
University of Reading
EARL RG6 .... **4**
University of Reading
EARL RG6 .... **4**
University of Reading
EARL RG6 .... **5**
University of Reading
READ RG1 .... **3**
University of Reading
READ RG1 .... **4**
University of Reading
WHIT RG2 .... **5**
Upcroft Primary School
TLHT RG30 .... **4**
Valley Road Primary School
HEN RG9 .... **15**
Waingels Copse School
WODY RG5 .... **36**
Walter County Infant School
WWKG RG41 .... **64**
Waverley School
EWKG RG40 .... **70**
Welfare Clinic
TLHT RG30 .... **39**
Wescott County Infants School
EWKG RG40 .... **65**
West Berkshire District Council
THLE RG7 .... **4**
Westende County Junior School
EWKG RG40 .... **65**
Western Elms Surgery
TLHT RG30 .... **4**
The West Street Practice
HEN RG9 .... **6**
Westwood Farm County
Junior School
CALC RG31 .... **31**
Westwood Road Health Centre
CALC RG31 .... **39**
Whitchurch Primary School
GOR/PANG RG8 .... **20**
White County Infants School
EWKG RG40 .... **65**
White House School
WWKG RG41 .... **64**
Whiteknights Cp School
EARL RG6 .... **51**
Whitley Park School
WHIT RG2 .... **50**
Whitley Villa Surgery
READ RG1 .... **42**
Whitley Wood Surgery
WHIT RG2 .... **60**
Wilson Junior & Infant School
TLHT RG30 .... **4**
Winnersh Cp School
WWKG RG41 .... **53**
Winterbourne House Clinic
TLHT RG30 .... **41**
Wokingham Child
Guidance Clinic
EWKG RG40 .... **64**
Wokingham Cricket Club
WWKG RG41 .... **64**
Wokingham Hospital
WWKG RG41 .... **64**
Wokingham Theatre
EWKG RG40 .... **54**
Wokingham Town Council
EWKG RG40 .... **64**
Woodley Centre Surgery
WODY RG5 .... **44**
Woodley C of E Primary School
WODY RG5 .... **45**
Woodley Park Estate 59-69
WODY RG5 .... **44**
Woodley Town Council
WODY RG5 .... **44**
Woodside Business Park
WHIT RG2 .... **60**
Woosehill Surgery
WWKG RG41 .... **64**
Works
WHIT RG2 .... **49**